THE ESSENCE OF ASTROLOGY

P. Khurrana has pursued the study of astrology, mantras, vaastu and tarot with great passion. A columnist and bestselling author whose work has been acknowledged worldwide, he is a devotee of Lord Shiva. He participates in the astro-based programme *Sitarre Ki Kehnde Ne* (Alpha TV Punjabi) and is advisor to several politicians, actors and business tycoons.

Those who know Astrology only indicate in a
way what will take place in the future.
Who else, except the Creator Brahma,
can say with certainty what
will definitely happen?

THE ESSENCE OF ASTROLOGY

P. Khurrana

RUPA

Published by
Rupa Publications India Pvt. Ltd. 2004
161-B/4, Gulmohar House,
Yusuf Sarai Community Centre,
New Delhi 110049

Sales centres:

Bengaluru Chennai
Hyderabad Kolkata Mumbai

P-ISBN: 978-81-291-0484-7
E-ISBN: 978-81-291-4301-3

Sixth impression 2026

10 9 8 7 6

Printed in India

Dedicated to Her Holiness
my mother, late Smt. Raj Khurrana

CONTENTS

FOREWORD

The extent to which we, on the basis of astrology, can locate our weaknesses and strengths, capabilities and potential, helps us shape the future accordingly. Every individual should therefore become cognisant of his or her natural capabilities and then, one can control and command its vigorous prosecution at the time of need.

Shakespeare says:

> There is a tide in the affairs of men,
> Which taken at the flood,
> Leads on to fortune;
> Omitted, all the voyage of their life
> Is bound in shallows.

Admittedly, men at times are masters of their fate. It is necessary therefore, that all should understand their inborn traits and skills in order to control and utilise them to the greatest advantage.

Your Sun Sign is a key to your inner self. By a careful application of the advice in this book you can mould your character and ability to greater purpose.

P. Khurrana has judiciously placed various information on zodiac signs focusing on career, health, profession and general traits of a person. Every individual of each zodiac sign has been given remedies including gem therapy, prayers, mantras, colour healing, favourable food and various other aspects to help shape his or her destiny. In fact, this book is the first work of its kind dealing with all possible aspects of the Sun Signs and the Moon Signs.

Swami S. Chandra

PREFACE

Astrology stands majestically on its own foundation, whether you call it science, fiction or mystic theory. It is a part of the Vedas, being one of its Angas. They were revealed by the ancient Rishis endowed with the knowledge of the present, the past and the future. There is more than one system involved. The commentators differ in their interpretation of the texts. The enunciations, the methodology and the conclusions are analysed with reference to the prevailing condition, situation, environment, etc. It requires considerable insight and intuition to interpret them to suit modern conditions and surroundings.

Astrology is a divine subject; a universal law consisting of nine planets which affects and shapes the future. Dr. F.W. Farzar has correctly quoted, "From the universal law of habit (inborn traits) little by little, day by day, act by act, thread by thread and link by link we mould the character, we weave the roof, we forge the chains which bind our being in forming our habits, we form our character." Nevertheless, it is quite possible that one can improve natural development by a careful application of astrological advice.

All over the world, astrology enjoys a place of great importance in the day-to-day affairs of people. The astrologer is consulted quite often, particularly on occasions like births, inauguration of business, matchmaking, conducting marriages, constructing houses and scores of other social, religious and spiritual activities. Religious observances are decided on astrological advice. Going a step further, we can even see people of divergent religious faiths consulting astrologers for finding solutions to problems or seeking their guidance in taking decisions. The process of consulting the astrologer starts as soon as a child is born, not only to know its future, but also the fortunes and misfortunes that are likely to visit the parents and close relatives. Even those who call themselves rationalists and declare their disbelief in astrology do not venture to finalise the marriages of their kin without getting astrological clearance. Above all, I have yet to see any film producer who performs the *mahurat* without astrological advice.

Who are the people who need the help of an astrologer? They are those whose lives have gone awry, who have some fear of disease, failure or death, who are worried about their parents, husbands, wives or children, who are curious about what the future holds, or those who are in deep trouble. To such persons, the astrologer is a silver lining in the dark clouds, a light in darkness.

The astrologer is expected to strengthen people by making predictions which will wipe away tears, generate smiles, boost morale, kindle hope, foster confidence and set people on the path of success. All said and done, it is better to approach the astrologer than to ruminate over one's misfortunes.

As a remedial measure for ill-luck, sincere prayers to God would prove highly beneficial, coupled with helping the needy to the extent possible.

Remedial measures work, like applied behavioural psychology. This, in fact, is like putting the *kriyaman* and *Agmi Karma* of the native into proper perspective for better living. He is encouraged to adopt the behaviour which is likely to do him maximum good. The remedial measures act mainly at the mystical level. For example, when the energy of a person is directed at highlighting his Jupiterian traits and subduing his Saturnine proclivities, he also starts to act in that way which may change his lifestyle tremendously.

Though this book is not a complete manual on astrology, it is my sincere attempt to make my lay readers understand the role of astrology. It contains all the necessary information on general astrological knowledge pertaining to your Sun Sign: love, relationships, mantra, yantra, fast, gems, lucky days, colours, etc. This book is a boon to people keen on getting acquainted with astrology. Both practitioners and amateurs can profit from the reading of this book and clear many confusions and doubts on the subject. It can also serve as a useful arsenal to enter into discussion with any astrologer one prefers to consult. The book will be an asset for ready reference and deserves to be possessed by all lovers of astrology.

P. KHURRANA

Office:
Hotel Shivalikview, Sector 17
Chandigarh
(0172) 2703018, 2712280
pkhurrana@astroindia.com

ARIES

THE RAM

(21st March – 20th April)
The Sign of the Warrior or Pioneer

- Governs the head.
- Planetary Ruler: Mars.
- Virtues: Active, enterprising, spontaneous, courageous.
- Vices: Violent, possessive, brutal, coarse, indecisive, egoistic and jealous.

ARIES (SUN SIGN)

Aries is symbolised by a Ram, which is by nature rash, combative, lascivious, springy and hardy. With Mars ruling this sign, people born under the sign of Aries are active, ambitious, bold, confident, courageous and impulsive. They are always interested in challenges and once they have achieved what they have sought, they move on to the next project. They possess a childlike naivete and must learn to cultivate patience and think before they act. They have an abundant amount of physical energy which should always be expressed. If it is not released, this energy is likely to emerge as aggression, anger and hostility.

Mars, the ancient symbol of war and action, strongly influences persons born in April, making the combative element predominate. As a rule, they fight their way through obstacles and dangers, experiencing many changes in their life and career.

Generally, the men born in this time of the year suffer a great deal through their affections. They seldom understand women and often make great mistakes in their relationships with them. They generally go to extremes and are too frank and outspoken and are prone to make enemies by want of tact. They are extremely ambitious. They succeed in life and either amass money or gain positions of responsibility.

People born during this period of the year have strong will power, ambition and courage. They do not like criticism, and lack tact and diplomacy. They are straightforward and do not care much for the feelings and sentiments of others. By nature, they are impulsive and rash. They usually succeed in life, achieve a good position and acquire money. They are best suited for a career connected with metals, e.g. metallurgy, engineering, surgery, explosives, sports and so on. Their love affairs are quick and sudden. However, they are usually unhappy in their married life because they seldom understand their partners.

Forceful and determined to get their own way, they can become indignant and even hot-tempered when opposed, although they soon forget an argument or a grudge. Since they are fond of having their own way, enjoy independence and are happy when in command, they may not be suited for occupations where they have to subjugate their desires. An excess of recklessness, impatience and lack of forethought may lead to personal calamity, so they should traïn themselves to think before they act.

ARIES (MOON SIGN)

MESHA (Chu, Che, Cho, La, Li, Lu, Le, Lo, Aa)

Mesh (Aries) ruled by Mars is a symbol of Ram. This is the sign of the go-getter whose enthusiasm is so great that it will inspire others to come along with him. Ariens like to be their own master. As a rule, Ariens are enterprising and enthusiastic, but somewhat unapproachable or hard to get, and any advice from others will fall on deaf ears. The ruling Mars endows the native with a highly fertile imagination, a temperament that varies constantly and an inclination to look at life from an imaginary point of view. It also makes him strange, restless and somewhat unsure of himself. This moon sign forms writers, poets and lawyers. It holds the possibility of second sight, causes sudden, reckless journeys by sea and gives more force of inertia rather than actual determination and perseverance.

If born during the day, the Mesha native will get unforeseen fortune which will enable him to release himself from problems. He is always hopeful and is able to endure in times of stress.

If born around sunset, it is unlucky for almost everything, since there is a deficiency of organising skills and bravery. This is an unfortunate situation and the native's impulsive nature will bring difficulties and he may go through several affairs and frustrating experiences in marriage.

Mesha in the ascendant, from the standpoint of character, gives ambition, moral and physical courage and energy, which enables the native to succeed through his own efforts. However, many problems can be avoided if the native tries to guard against being too impatient, egoistic and violent.

ARIES – YOUR PERSONAL OUTLOOK

The Aries-born has a middle-sized, strong, muscular body and round eyes. He or she is active and independent. He or she is bold, capable, stubborn, frank and ambitious. He or she is also sensitive, talkative, respectable and fond of beauty and art. Spouse is inclined to be lazy and proud. An Arien is likely to have the following features:

- Dry hair
- Freckled face
- Aquiline nose
- Baldness at the temples
- Premature white hair

ARIES – YOUR OCCULT FOUNDATION

Aries is ruled by Mars whose occult value is nine. The number nine has polarised positive and negative associations. In its positive aspects, nine is the number of spiritual and mental achievement. The Hebrews considered it to be the number of truth, because when multiplied it reproduces itself. In Kabbalism, it represents the foundation. As the triple Triad, it is the incorruptible number of fulfillment and attainment. In the Eleusinian mysteries, there were nine spheres through which the consciousness had to pass before it could be born anew. It is also the number of man, symbolising the nine months of gestation before birth. Because of its composition of equal threes, nine has associations with the triangle.

FINANCE AND PROFESSION

They will have great ability in making money in all forms of industry, business organisation or in the employment of others. They will always see a way out of any difficulty and be self-reliant and determined in whatever course of action they may decide to follow. They will be fearless and courageous, but perhaps too headstrong for their own good. They will speculate on a large scale in all they undertake. They will treat life more as a game than from a serious standpoint. As a general rule, luck will favour them during the greater part of their life.

Professions connected with Ariens are army, defence department, surgeons, police, chemists, law, occupations involving iron and steel, factories, industries or sports goods.

HEALTH AND FOOD

They will be endowed with a splendid constitution and great vitality. They will recover quickly from any illness. Their greatest danger will come from accidents of all kinds, especially those caused by firearms, fires, explosions, road accidents . Normally they suffer from health problems like cuts, wounds, sore eyes, boils, burns, blood pressure, piles, itches, fractures, urinary complaints, jaundice, slow coagulation of blood, tumours, epilepsy.

They will also be prone to high blood pressure, heart disease and apoplexy.

The following food should be included in their diet:

- Potato
- Carrot
- Onion
- Apple
- Fish

They should avoid tomato and red meat.

ARIES AS A LOVER

Male

The male Arien lover is extremely frank, enthusiastic in love and practical. He demands your best at all times and does not hesitate to let you know when you are slipping. Adventure and freedom are the best points of this lover. He is of dominating nature and will follow so fast behind you that you will not go very far. He is romantic, rash, passionate and a spendthrift.

He is compatible with:

Aries:	Sex, love, business, friendship.
Gemini:	Sex, love and friendship.
Sagittarius:	Sex, love, marriage, business and lasting friendship.
Aquarius:	A long friendship.

He is incompatible with:

Taurus
Virgo

Female

This lover is witty, intelligent and independent. She expects praise from you and good care. She will have the power to boss over you, and can be aggressive but very romantic and sexy. Fiery in passion, she can be controlled with tact and patience. She wants freedom before and after marriage and you have to trust her because she will be faithful.

She is compatible with:

Gemini: Sex, love and friendship.
Leo: Love, marriage, business partnership.
Libra: Sex but not marriage, friendship.
Pisces: Romantic, loving and strong friendship, good for marriage.

She is incompatible with:

Taurus
Cancer
Virgo
Scorpio

YOUR RELATIONSHIPS

Love is power.

To love or to be in love – the choice may come to all of us. Both ways may lead to the same end, in time – through pain, when happiness would mean bondage. No one can deliberately choose what he or she is not ready for, is not able or willing to accept. If this be the case, circumstances are allowed to choose for us. We have to learn to live, for a time at least with this choice – which we, as individuals, have not had the courage to make.

Love and marriage are two words of vital importance to the average young man or woman. Both words are correlated to physical compatibility.

Compatibility is a manifestation of the principles of duality and of the 'pairs of opposites' which form the basis of the created universe as we know it.

Our emotions and moods vary according to our Sun Sign when we are concerned about love and marriage. In fact, our Seventh House governs romance and establishes our marriage traits and potential, but the Sun in alliance with Venus influences, for the Sun Sign supplies a wealth of love in those whose birth dates occurs in a particular zodiac sign. Thus, Sun Signs are closely connected with our love and sex life. At the end of each combination is given astro advice which can keep love refreshed and new.

Aries with Aries

Fire with Fire is a compatible combination, although it produces a volatile, exciting and sometimes stressful atmosphere. Peace, quiet and relaxation will be difficult to achieve. If both people try to rule the roost or compete, disputes and tension will result. When necessary, each will defend the other. Their arch enemy – boredom – will seldom arise in this duo because both like to be active. There will be seldom any deception, pretence or hypocrisy. Both partners provide protection to each other. These two are capable of reaching the far heavens of happiness, since they both require essentially love and sex.

Astro Advice

- Wear coral of four rattis.
- Avoid wearing red clothes while meeting.

Aries with Taurus

Fire with Earth is not an easy combination and since the needs and natures of these signs are so different, there will be difficulties without compromise. Aries needs the stimulus of new enterprises or challenges, but Taurus prefers quiet stability. Aries becomes impatient with the Taurean's slowness and stay-put attitude. Aries can help a Taurean with his or her schemes and ideas and in return Taurus can assist the Arien to come out of impractical ideas.

Astro Advice

- Wear diamond of two carats.
- The woman should wear pink clothes.

Aries with Gemini

Fire with Air is an agreeable combination and, since both generate a lively atmosphere, life is not boring. Gemini's wits can match the Aries fighting spirit. Both enjoy variety, action, discovery and new things, so they should share their interests. Together they have a better chance of harmony and can fulfil their dreams. Sexually too, they will be ideally mated.

Astro Advice

- Avoid all intoxicants and non-vegetarian food.
- Lucky stones are pukhraj and emerald.

Aries with Cancer

Fire with Water can create problems unless they search for common ground. Cancer is sensitive and often hurt by the frank, abrupt or even abrasive ways of Aries. Aries does not appreciate Cancer's sentimentality and emotional moods. Remember, Cancer is a cardinal sign of leadership. It is a tricky problem because when you have two leaders, how do you determine which one will follow whom? It seems like an impossible situation but there is a solution. They can walk side by side, with no one ahead and no one behind.

Astro Advice

- The man should wear pearl and woman should wear coral.
- Avoid long drives.

Aries with Leo

Fire with Fire is a positive combination and provided they do not both try to be the boss, this can be a stimulating duo. Leo can appreciate the Aries drive and initiative while Aries is not overwhelmed by the big ideas, power and largesse of Leo. Both signs are outgoing, extroverted, warm and vibrant. Leos are born to command; if this comes in the Aries mind and both join hands in friendship, the relationship works like a charm. But the trouble is, Aries may not endorse Leo's views.

Astro Advice

- The man should wear pukhraj and woman should wear ruby.
- Avoid wearing pink while going out for dinner.

Aries with Virgo

Fire is volatile and impetuous, whereas Earth is practical, stable and self-controlled. There is a great contrast of temperaments here. Aries cannot be bothered with the method, fuss and attention to detail which comes so naturally to Virgo, although Aries appreciates the results. Emotional natures differ so much that a good mental affinity is vital. Both of them lean towards purity of purpose.

Astro Advice

- The man should wear coral and woman should wear emerald.
- Saturday and Tuesdays are auspicious for outings.

Aries with Libra

Fire has a natural affinity with Air, but since theses signs are opposite to each other in the zodiac, they can repel as well as attract. If conflicts arise, Aries triumphs while Libra becomes upset or leaves. Initially there is often a strong physical and emotional attraction between these two. In this relationship, the latter will remain cool and stable but when the Aries aggressiveness becomes intolerable, expect a thunderstorm. The Librans give Aries courage and more balanced and tolerant inner drive, while the Arien inspires the Libran to turn his or her indecision into a firmer purpose.

Astro Advice

- The man should focus on his beloved.
- The woman should dress up in pure white sari with a golden border.

Aries with Scorpio

Fire with Water creates a highly charged association. Mars rules both signs, so there may be mutual appreciation of strength and capabilities or fierce competition. Forthright Aries does not suspect the secretive ways of Scorpio. Excellent for teamwork if goals agree, but these signs will demand much of each other. Aries may become unnaturally introverted and self-effacing. In happier associations, Aries will respond beautifully to Scorpio's strength, provided Scorpio keeps an open mind to the Aries' free and friendly approach to life.

Astro Advice

- Focus on good habits and avoid intoxication.
- Maintain diet and fitness routines.

Aries with Sagittarius

Fire does not conflict with Fire but, because they are both independent, they must allow each other some freedom.

Sagittarius encourages enthusiastic Aries who appreciates the sign's optimistic outlook and honesty. This is a fast tempo combination, so there is little peace and relaxation. Neither will tolerate the other being bossy. Both are happier when they are mentally and physically active. Despite their frequent squabbles, the idealistic Sagittarian moves the Aries to spontaneous affection.

Astro Advice

- The man should trust his beloved.
- The woman should wear clothes with stripes or checks.
- Wear coral of five carats.

Aries with Capricorn

This combination of Fire with Earth can be stressful, especially since Aries' ruling planet Mars is impetuous, impatient and fiery and Capricorn's ruler Saturn is cautious, sombre, slow and deliberate. Capricorn likes to plan ahead and can play a waiting game. Aries acts immediately and hates to wait. Unless both people are willing to exercise tolerance, their extremely different viewpoints can bring tension or even bitterness. Capricorn often unwittingly squashes Aries. Aries would be wise to cultivate and participate in discussions for it can aid him or her in keeping Capricorn's interest and their love making very much alive. Although Capricorn is not usually highly sexed, the experience will mean a great deal to him or her and offence is taken quickly if he or she is rejected on flimsy excuses.

Astro Advice

- The man should always think positively.
- Each should be allowed to handle their situations without the other's interference.

Aries with Aquarius

Fire is compatible with Air, but the interaction of the ruling planets – Mars for Aries and Uranus for Aquarius – can generate tremendous power, so much will depend on whether it is used constructively. Aquarius will not dampen the initiative and independence of Aries, while Aries appreciates a friend in Aquarius. Aries loves anything new, so is interested in the Aquarian's offbeat ways. But if Aquarius becomes unpredictable at an inopportune moment, Aries will be irritated and impatient.

Astro Advice

- The woman should wear coral of five carats.
- The woman should show her love and true feelings to her lover/husband.
- The man should wear black stone of four carats on the ring finger.

Aries with Pisces

Their ruling planets, Fiery Mars and Watery Neptune, are entirely different in nature. If they are true to their sign types, they are worlds apart and it will be difficult to find a common ground. Positive, active Aries cannot fathom the nebulous mysterious substance of Pisces, who often irritates by appearing to be negative or indecisive. The Piscean will always look up to Aries and has something important to learn. Sexually, the Piscean is adaptable but being sensitive, cannot take criticism in this direction.

Astro Advice

- Porcelain figures of Venus and Jasmine should be kept in the south-west corner of the bedroom.
- The man should wear yellow sapphire of seven carats on the index finger.
- The woman may find it necessary to bend to a stronger point of view.

ASTRO GUIDE

How to improve your luck

Lucky Date: 9th, 18th, 27th of any month.

Lucky Day: Tuesday for meetings, Monday for love and romance.

Lucky Colour: Red, pink and crimson. These should be used as the colour of curtains, bed sheets and walls. Attire should match the lucky colour.

Lucky Gem: Coral of 8-10 rattis on Tuesday evening after Pran Pratishta (prayer to Mars).
Blood stone.
Ruby of four rattis on Sunday after Pran Pratishta (prayer to Sun).

Lucky Metal: Gold and copper.

Lucky Flower: Red rose, lily.
Mantra: Aum Kran Krin Kron Se Bhomaye Namah.
Lucky Talisman: Copper or gold key should be worn next to skin or the following Yantra:

7	2	9
8	6	4
3	10	5

TAURUS

THE BULL

(21st April – 21st May)
The Sign of the Builder or Producer

- Governs the neck and throat.
- Planetary Ruler: Venus.
- Virtues: Loyal, generous, trustworthy, stable and practical.
- Vices: Possessive, coarse, lazy, prejudiced and limited in outlook.

TAURUS (SUN SIGN)

Venus, the ruler of Taurus endows these people with kindness, patience, charm and fondness. People born during this period of the year are dominating and obstinate. They are practical, successful and trustworthy. They are generally patient and persevering and have great power of endurance. Taureans make faithful and loyal friends. They are very careful about their personal comfort and money matters. A native whose Sun is in Taurus is a sensuous person, and very jealous and sentimental in matters of sex. They can be easily misled by emotions and affections.

They are sensual, extremely passionate, possessive and jealous. They are straightforward and direct and ponder for a long time before taking a decision. Once they have a goal in mind, however, they are almost obsessive about attaining it. They are even-tempered and while it takes some time before anger is ignited, their temper can be vile and difficult to control.

They are extremely social and most happy when entertaining their friends, or those they love. They make splendid hosts or hostesses; they have great taste in food, and in an emergency make excellent cooks. They are artistic in their homes, wonderful in their arrangement of furniture and make things appeal.

As a rule they are often considered richer than they really are, and are more or less showy in everything they do.

They are governed largely by their emotions and sensations but affection has a greater hold on them than passion.

Like the bull, they are slow to anger but, when finally stirred up, they are capable of violent outbursts. They are stubborn in the face of all opposition, resisting any compromise.

TAURUS (MOON SIGN)

VRIKH (E, U, A, O, V, Vi, Vr, Ve, Vo)

Taurus (Vrikh) symbolised by the 'bull' is persevering and musical. The Moon sign is fortunate on the whole but more so, in matters of love and affection and financial issues. It make the native soft, slightly delicate, understanding and his disposition prompts him to search for calm and quiet and go for strolls by the lake or sea. The voice sounds soothing to the ears, however may be spoilt early in life and there may be chances of throat problems.

Those born in early hours show inconstancy, infidelity or envy.

Those born in midday signifies travel, however related with problems. It also signifies changes and modifications in matters of love.

A birth during sunset is a definite indicator of prosperity for artists.

From the moral standpoint the influence is benefic. The native is steadfast, persevering, firm and gentle. If anger is aroused, he becomes very violent. His ideals, though not especially noble, are not materialistic. He is a good listener and can keep his own counsel, so that even if his education is not superior, he can acquire a certain degree of veneer as he advances in years, thanks to his adaptability.

This position indicates progress in worldly matters through the native's own efforts. He has a practical and organising mind, and is equally well suited for business as for the management of property, or for a political career.

TAURUS – YOUR PERSONAL OUTLOOK

Taurus-born persons are of short to middle stature, have a broad forehead, bright eyes, thick and stout neck, dark hair, clear complexion, well-developed body. Following are their characteristics:

- Prominent and watery eyes
- Long lashes
- Thick eyebrows
- Thick neck
- Hands and feet are short and broad

TAURUS – YOUR OCCULT FOUNDATION

Taurus is ruled by Venus whose occult value is six. The number of equilibrium, as well as balance, harmony, health and time. The six-sided figure, the hexagon, is formed by the union of two triangles. In addition this union represents marriage and the hermaphrodite, both of which are the result of the union of the male and female. The Pythagoreans considered six the form of forms, the perfection of all the parts, and associated it with immortality. In Christian symbolism too, six is the number of perfection because God created the world in six days. In Kabbalism, six represents beauty and creation. In shapes, six is represented by the hexagram, the symbol of the union of opposites.

FINANCE AND PROFESSION

Taureans being economical will accumulate and hoard money and never squander unnecessarily. Gambling nature is also indicated. A Taurean is of materialistic mind, will get money from others, is practical and will rise gradually, will take chances and risk money.

Venus is positively ruling which stands for art, beauty, culture, charm, clothes. So they will be successful where harmony and rhythm go together. Singers, fashion designers, hoteliers, interior decorators, charmers and magicians come under this zodiac sign.

Any trade concerning comfort, cosmetics, furnishings, gems, hair dressing, hospitality, jewellery, match making, modelling would be successful.

Persons born under this sign are also good surgeons, chemists, exporters, film directors, religious leaders, healers, astrologers and excellent public servants.

HEALTH AND FOOD

They will start life with an excellent constitution, but owing to a tendency towards luxury and good living, they will be inclined to dig their own grave.

They will have a slender, symmetrical form in their early years which they are likely to ruin as they advance in life by over-indulgence in sweet stuffs or the good things of the table.

They will be liable to flattery, degeneration of the heart and a dropsical condition in their later years, but such things are in their own power to control. There may also be some tendency towards problems relating to the lungs, bronchial tubes and throat.

The following food should be included in their diet:

- Almond
- Cabbage
- Egg yolk

They should avoid non-vegetarian food, red meat and sugar.

TAURUS AS A LOVER

Male

He is devoted to you and is reliable, generous and faithful. Sincere in situations of love, opposition and upsetting conditions. Not impulsive in love, but responds well to kind treatment.

He is compatible with:

Taurus:	Physically, an excellent union.
Cancer:	Romance, marriage, business and lasting friendship.
Virgo:	Romance, sex, marriage, business and long lasting friendship.
Scorpio:	Friendship, sex but not marriage.
Pisces:	Sex and great friendship.

He is incompatible with:

Aries
Libra
Aquarius

Female

She is of doubtful nature, anxious to lead a happy domestic life. Sincere in love and peace loving, social, affectionate. When opposed, she becomes stubborn and unyielding. Usually secretive and reserved.

She is compatible with:

Cancer:	Romance, marriage, business and lasting friendship.
Sagittarius:	A great friendship, sex.
Capricorn:	Romance, sex, marriage, business and long lasting friendship.
Pisces:	Sex and great friendship.

She is incompatible with:

Aries
Gemini
Leo

YOUR RELATIONSHIPS

Taurus with Taurus

Earth with Earth produces a stable conservative, down-to-earth association and this relationship has enduring qualities because both want to maintain the status quo. This also can lead to a lifestyle which seems stodgy to the more adventurous type. When provoked, both can be jealous and possessive. Because both people are cautious and conscious of security, this team lacks dynamic initiative.

Astro Advice

- The man should wear diamond of one carat.
- Soft manners and smiles are the greatest charm of the woman.

Taurus with Gemini

Taurus is the most Earthy sign of all, while Airy Gemini is restless, volatile and changeable. Their basic needs and motives are opposed. Gemini's love of constant change and variety can be unsettling for Taurus who likes to stay put. It will be an impossible mission if Taurus should try to possess Gemini.

Astro Advice

- The man should wear a thin gold bracelet or ring.
- The woman should use bright coloured nail polish while going to meet the beloved.

Taurus with Cancer

The natural affinity between Earth and Water means that both will have much in common. Feelings, emotions and affection are important to both signs and Taurus appreciates the attention and protection which Cancer enjoys giving. Both are basically conservative, so conflicts are unlikely to be caused by extreme or divergent interests. Common-sense and logical discussions are the best antidotes when over emotionalism develops.

Astro Advice

- The man should focus on diet and exercise.
- Telling lies can create problems for the man.

Taurus with Leo

Earth with Fire in two such strong-willed signs cause conflicts and opposition unless both practise compromise. Leo thrives on the attention and affection Taurus naturally dishes out. Taurus often tolerates being dominated by Leo until, one day, the worm turns. Leo's big ideas can be disturbing to conservative Taurus.

Astro Advice

- The man should wear ruby of six rattis.
- The woman should not compare her beloved with anyone.

Taurus with Virgo

Earth with Earth means that both can see eye to eye in many ways and both are practical, realistic, capable and thorough. However, their emotions are very dissimilar. Taurus is deeply emotional and possessive. Virgo's feelings are more under control. Their goals will have much in common because both desire material success and security.

Astro Advice

- The woman should not hide anything from the beloved.
- The man should wear diamond of one carat.

Taurus with Libra

Although there is a little affinity between Earth and Air, Venus creates a strong link because it rules both signs. A bond will depend on feelings and affection or mutual appreciation of beauty and the finer things of life. This is because peace and harmony are very important to both signs. Neither one is likely to provoke conflict. Diplomatic Libra can tactfully manipulate stubborn Taurus. Both need their pleasures and little luxuries, so more than a shoestring budget will be necessary for such a team. There's hardly a square foot of space in or around the home where they will disagree.

Astro Advice

- The man should curb his habit of overspending.
- The woman should impress her beloved by giving small gifts.

Taurus with Scorpio

Although Earth is compatible with Water, these are opposite signs in the zodiac. In love relationships, this factor often brings irresistible physical attraction initially but when this diminishes, the pendulum can swing the other way unless they have more things in common. Both are jealous and possessive, so mutual trust is essential. Such intense feelings can sometimes bring about a turbulent love-hate relationship. They both have a tendency to be reserved with strangers and neither is inclined to make long speeches unless they have something important to say.

Astro Advice

- The man should dress up in casual wear and stripes will suit him.
- The woman should dress up in traditional wear with a red bindi on the forehead.

Taurus with Sagittarius

This combination of Earth and Fire is as different as chalk and cheese. Taurus is the most stable sign and only feels secure when life is settled. The strong desire to stay put and possess the loved one may be at odds with the Sagittarian who needs to feel free and independent. The Fire sign is restless, enjoys changes, likes distant horizons, faraway places and needs plenty of room both mentally and physically. Too much of this will prove very unsettling for Taurus. But true love can still manage to transcend all these differences.

Astro Advice

- The woman should wear trendy clothes to impress her lover.

- The man should avoid fickle love for the sake of personal gains.

Taurus with Capricorn

This combination of Earth is compatible as security-conscious Taurus will always appreciate Capricorn's practical attitude, perseverance, realistic approach and ambition. Both are conservative, patient and willing to share responsibilities. Neither places any real importance on superficial pleasure, so life could be just too serious at times.

Astro Advice

- The man should respond vibrantly to the feelings and ideas of his beloved.
- The woman should wear blue sapphire of five rattis on Saturday after Pran Pratishta (prayer to Saturn).

Taurus with Aquarius

Earth and Air have little in common in this combination of two extremely determined signs which are separate in nature. Taurus will not understand the Aquarian's unpredictability who wants to live free and aloof with a natural desire to share affection with many people but Taurus takes another track and is much more exclusive about feelings. The Aquarian makes friends in five seconds while the bull takes years.

Astro Advice

- The man should show his feelings by giving gifts and cards.

- The woman should wear trendy clothes to impress her lover.

Taurus with Pisces

This combination of Earth and Water is very compatible because the ruling planets, Venus and Jupiter, do not clash. Lots of friendship, affection or love can be shared and they both appreciate beauty, artistry, pleasure and the good things of life. Each can help to balance the other because Taurus is practical whereas Pisces is often up in the clouds; the realist complements the dreamer.

Astro Advice

- The man should be wary of a beloved who suddenly presents him with unsolicited ideas for consideration.
- The woman should avoid junk food.
- The man should try not to go to the beloved in casual wear.

ASTRO GUIDE

How to improve you luck

Lucky Date: 6th, 15th, 24th and 3rd, 12th, 21st, 30th of any month.

Lucky Day: Friday for love and romance. Thursday for meetings.

Lucky Colour: Blue, royal blue and pink. These should be used as curtains, bed sheets and as colour of wall. Attire should also match the lucky colour.

Lucky Gem:	Diamond of two rattis on Friday morning after Pran Pratishtha. Zircon or white sapphire of five rattis on Friday morning after Pran Pratishtha.
Lucky Metal:	Silver, copper, platinum and any white metal.
Lucky Flower:	Lotus, white rose.
Mantra:	Aum Hran Hrin Hraon Sha Shukrai Namah.
Lucky Talisman:	Engrave figure '5' in gold and wear next to the skin.

GEMINI

THE TWINS

(22nd May – 21st June)
The Sign of the Artist or Inventor

- Governs the hands, lungs, arms and respiratory system.
- Planetary Ruler: Mercury.
- Virtues:Reliable, intelligent, clever, expressive, ambitious.
- Vices: Nervous, restless, changeable.

GEMINI (SUN SIGN)

As a Mercury ruled Air sign, Gemini rules mental energy. Gemini natives are adaptable, extremely intelligent and quick witted. Persons born during this period possess a dual character and temperament. Their moods are easily changeable and as a rule they are restless, diplomatic and ambitious. Being intellectual and versatile, they are suitable for a variety of careers. including teaching, journalism, publishing, selling and acting. People with the Sun in Gemini are inconsistent in their love life. By nature they are flirtatious and have more than one affair. One of their difficulties is an inability to concentrate and a constant need for instant gratification which causes them to give up rather easily. With difficult aspects they can be too scattered, restless and insensitive.

Persons born in this sign derive much satisfaction from work accomplished, for their nature always has the tendency to subject it to severe criticsm afterwards. Such persons often attain a prominent position in the centre of some progressive moment, but they generally follow two professions, one to suit the public and the other to suit themselves.

Their personality is extremely fascinating and they leave their mark everywhere.

In matters of affection they are a great mystery. They can love passionately and yet be unfaithful at the same time. They often keeps two homes and usually by their wonderful tact escape being found out. They make lots of friends and are kind-hearted.

They often have great ups and downs but nothing makes much impression on them. If they are depressed one moment they may be equally gay the next. They change their outlook on life many times during their career, but if they change their feelings of affections for a person, it is as if that person for them has ceased to exist.

Their versatile mind make them learn a little about a lot of things, so there is a danger of becoming a jack of all trades but master of none, unless they focus on a particular career.

They have the symmetrical influence of the Gemini insofar as they are genereous in an academic kind way of way, but emotionally they lack deep feelings when compared with the scale of emotional responses possible for some of the other zodiac signs. Perhaps this is a reason why a fair percentage of people born with Gemini on the ascendant have a problem in marriage or marry more then once.

GEMINI (MOON SIGN)

MITHUN (K, Ki, Ku, Gh, Dh, Ch, Ke, Ko, H)

Gemini is a double-sided sign and shows itself in a split personality. Sometimes it signifies carelessness and rash deeds, frequently idle meaningless chatter. It bestows the native with great intelligence and he is inclined towards the academic pursuit of literature, history and geography. Numerous short trips will occur. Life will be long but interrupted by several disputes, despite the native's desire for peace and quiet.

Gemini appearing to be fickle indicates unfaithfulness with someone who is close to the native, frequently a relative.

Situated in 20° of Gemini, it brings a great number of educated acquaintances who shall enable the native to progress and grow.

A certain perception in everything will enable the native to learn quickly. His visual memory is excellent, but he cannot remember names, unless the Moon occupies the sign. The defect of those born with Gemini in the ascendant is that they are shy, lack self-confidence, and do not push themselves forward, in spite of their innate pride and ambition.

Success often comes through this sign, and the native progresses through his own merit, although luck, of which he knows how to avail himself in his own interests, often helps him. He is usually practical, without despising idealistic things. He is a man of refined tastes and a lover of beautiful things, but he also appreciates the money which can procure them.

GEMINI – YOUR PERSONAL OUTLOOK

A Gemini-born has a slender, beautiful body, curly hair and prominent nose. He is clever, fickle and fond of sensual pleasure. He is good conversationalist. He does not usually maintain good relations with his own relatives. Spouse may be ill-tempered and unkind. Following are the general characteristics of Geminis:

- Dark hair
- Fair skin
- Clear voice
- They walk and move quickly
- Well-developed muscles and long limbs

GEMINI – YOUR OCCULT FOUNDATION

Gemini is ruled by Mercury whose occult value is five. This number symbolises the physical man and his five senses and thus connotes sensuality and pleasure. It also resonates with higher qualities; it is a man with his four limbs plus a head, the four cardinal points with the centre, the four elements plus a fifth element of ether, the universal vitalising substance that permeates all things. In this respect, five is the number of hierophant. Since five divides the perfect number 10 equally into two parts, it represents equilibrium and balance.

FINANCE AND PROFESSION

This is a difficult sign to interpret. In matters of finance, Gemini is quick-witted and clever. They have brains which gives them great opportunities. At times they are likely to be very rich and at other times the reverse.

When they have money they will be extravagant, and when they do not have, they can adapt themself to the lowliest sphere. In fact, the greatest danger is that they are by nature too adaptable to others as well as to conditions.

If they make the effort to hold their nature in check, they will easily become a success in whatever enterprise, industry, or work they associate with. This is a remarkably good sign for all who have to come before the public.

Geminians have interest in varied jobs as they are active, alert and industrious. Being good speakers, intelligent and humorous, they are fit for politics. They also make excellent brokers, share market agents, businessmen, secretaries, scientists and advocates. They also can be journalists, travelling agents.

HEALTH AND FOOD

Healthwise they will be inclined to be their own worst enemy. They will have an excellent constitution, but of the highly strung type. They will take too much out of themself in every possible way. They will be prone to live on their nerves and crave for change and travel. In order to "keep going" they will be liable at times to indulge in stimulants which will injure their digestive organs. As they will desist from following rules and regulations, they will not be inclined to be regular in their habits, but may eat at any time of the day and night and only sleep as and when they can.

In this way they are likely to break up the splendid constitution they would otherwise have. They will be liable to have trouble brought on by 'nerves,' twitching of the eyelids, some defect in the tongue or speech, blood disorders, eczema and skin eruptions. They should not nibble at food, should eat regularly and learn to relax.

The following food should be included in their diet:

- Red meat
- Fish
- Egg
- Plums
- Oranges

They should avoid smoking.

GEMINI AS A LOVER

Males

He feels that variety is the spice of life. He makes quick friendships, finds faults with others and loses them, so he cannot find a permanent friendship. He is the most difficult lover to hold and keep. He cannot be understood easily. Calculating and cynical in love, do not ask for any commitment from him. Best way to arouse him is to become disinterested in him, yet friendly. He is quite impersonal.

He is compatible with:

Aries: Sex, love and friendship.
Libra: Romance, love, marriage, business and long lasting friendship.

He is incompatible with:

Taurus
Scorpio

Capricorn
Aquarius

Female

She is intelligent and wants mental companionship. She cannot tolerate any opposition to her wishes and plans, cannot easily be imposed upon. If a situation arises she can leave you or the home.

She is compatible with:

Aries:	Sex, love and friendship.
Gemini:	Romance, marriage, business and lasting friendship.
Leo:	Romance, sex, marriage, business and long lasting friendship.
Pisces:	A shaky union for marriage but good for friendship and sex.

She is incompatible with:

Cancer
Virgo
Sagittarius
Capricorn

YOUR RELATIONSHIPS

Gemini with Gemini

This double dose of such a highly strung, restless Air sign ensures that life will never be dull or dreary. The relationship can be lively, excitable, scatterbrained, gossipy, intellectually stimulating, multipurpose, full of change, variety, interest or nervous tension. Who is going to be stuck with the phone bill though?

Gemini is an Air sign, ruled by Mercury, whose symbol is the twins. Two Geminis may occasionally block each other's vision of life but they understand each other's need for freedom. When a pair of twins tangle their temperaments, things do get criss-crossed. This combination brings with it the unique satisfaction of knowing a person like oneself.

Astro Advice

- The man should be loyal and faithful towards his beloved.
- The woman should dress up in pink or sky blue while going to meet her beloved.

Gemini with Cancer

The Air sign Gemini is mentally oriented whereas the Water elements of Cancer emphasise the emotions, so there is a marked contrast in natures. Variety, the spice of life to a Gemini, can make Cancer feel unsettled. Cancer's sentimentality and emotionalism will not evoke a deep response in Gemini who, in turn, never has time to fathom Cancer's moodiness. Gemini is also constantly busy so that Cancer sometimes will feel neglected.

Astro Advice

- The man should wear pearl of six rattis on Monday after Pran Pratishta (prayer to Moon).

- The woman should wear a thin gold bracelet or gold chain.

Gemini with Leo

Air with Fire will help maintain interest between these two signs, particularly on a mental or intellectual level. Leo likes to be the centre of attraction but may feel neglected when Gemini becomes absorbed in many interests or activities. Leo's 'think big' philosophy appeals to Gemini's mind. Leo's desire to take control may overpower Gemini's free spirit. If each person is happy to let the other go his or her own way, this can be a sparkling combination.

Astro Advice

- The woman should carry a bunch of flowers to cherish her beloved.
- The man should wear emerald of five rattis on Wednesday after Pran Pratishta (prayer to Mercury).

Gemini with Virgo

Although Air has little affinity with Earth, Mercury rules both signs and this can be a stimulating catalyst. Neither is over emotional, so common ground will include practical, social, mental or business interests. Realistic and systematic, Virgo will not always go along with Gemini's multitude plans or scatterbrained ideas, since Virgo concentrates more on one point.

Astro Advice

- The man should improve his tolerance power.

- It is best for the woman to observe silence during/over heated discussions.

Gemini with Libra

Air with Air is compatible in this combination which blends Mercury, the planet of the mind, with Venus, the symbol of love and emotion. This creates a mutual appreciation of all that is refined, artistic, beautiful, sociable, interesting, informative. Gemini likes to communicate, so is happy to share ideas with Libra who, in turn, is not fulfilled or complete when alone.

Astro Advice

- The man should wear white stone of 10 rattis on Monday after Pran Pratishta (prayer to Moon).
- The woman should wear emerald of three rattis on Wednesday after Pran Pratishta (prayer to Mercury).

Gemini with Scorpio

Air and Water will not be easy to mix in this combination of signs which are as different as black and white. Gemini lacks the deep emotional intensity of Scorpio and will be overwhelmed by such magnetic power. Gemini's free spirit will feel stifled if Scorpio becomes jealous and possessive.

The twins may never meet a Scorpio without a third person introducing them. They do not normally have enough in common to feel any vibrations across a room.

Astro Advice

- Both need to develop faith in each other.
- The woman should apply light colour mascara.

Gemini with Sagittarius

Air with Fire is a stimulating combination but, since these are opposite signs in the zodiac, not only can they attract each other but also repel. Gemini is self-contained enough to appreciate the Sagittarian's love for freedom and independence. Both are naturally busy, active people who like to fill their lives with interests, so a mutual exchange comes easily to them.

Astro Advice

- The woman should share responsibilities with her lover.
- The man should avoid fickle love.

Gemini with Capricorn

Although Air and Earth are very different, the young-at-heart spirit of Gemini can complete the wisdom and experience of Capricorn, provided both are willing to communicate. Sometimes they will have to agree to disagree because Gemini often changes direction, whereas Capricorn pursues a goal to its conclusion. Capricorn, steady and controlled, does not always understand the highly strung, quicksilver ways of Gemini. Although very different, each can enrich the other only with unique gifts and sensibility.

Astro Advice

- To impress his beloved, the man needs to show his good sense.
- The woman needs to wear a matching head gear with her dress.

Gemini with Aquarius

Air with Air is compatible, but their ruling planets, Mercury and Saturn, give very different natures and viewpoints. Gemini can accept a detached or unpredictable mood from Aquarius and is mentally stimulated by his/her originality and inventiveness. The unconventional and changeable quality of this relationship helps to keep it interesting.

Astro Advice

- The man should wear black stone of eight rattis on Saturday after Pran Pratishta (prayer to Saturn).
- The woman should trust her beloved.

Gemini with Pisces

The marked contrast between Air and Water is clearly illustrated in the great difference between their natures and outlooks. Gemini is logical, factual and mentally oriented, whereas Pisces is imaginative, dreamy and sensitive and lives by feelings, emotions, impressions and intuitions. Gemini may be unable to see reason in the illogical ways of Pisces. However, both signs are reasonably adaptable and tolerant of other people's ideas. Although they will very seldom understand each other's driving force, they will usually accept each other. Gemini is practical, quick and efficient but Pisces often dithers or is irritatingly indecisive.

Astro Advice

- The man should wear yellow sapphire of six carats on the index finger on Thursday after Pran Pratishta (prayer to Jupiter).
- The woman should use light colour lipstick and tie her hair in a bun.

ASTRO GUIDE

How to improve your luck

Lucky Date: All Series of 5 i.e. 5th, 15th, 25th, 30th.
Lucky Day: Wednesday for meetings, Friday for love and romance.
Lucky Colour: Green, ivory. These should be used as curtains, bed sheets and as colour of wall. Attire should also match the lucky colour.
Lucky Metal: Silver, gold.
Lucky Flower: Balm, celery, lavender.
Mantra: Aum Bran Brin Bron Se: Budhaye Namah.
Lucky Talisman: Engrave figure '5' in gold and wear next to skin.

CANCER

THE CRAB

(22nd June – 22nd July)
The Sign of the Prophet or Teacher

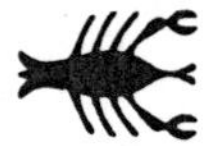

- Governs the stomach and digestive system.
- Planetary Ruler: Moon.
- Virtues: Sensitive, motherly and patient.
- Vices: Changeable, overanxious and lazy.

CANCER (SUN SIGN)

This sign is symbolised by a Crab and the ruling planet, the Moon, provides Cancerians with a fertile imagination, moodiness and an inclination towards high emotions.

Persons born during this period are changeable, sensitive, moody and restless. They are emotional, tenacious in their feelings and attached to their home and family. However they seldom find domestic happiness. Being hardworking and industrious they are usually successful in business. They often reach a high position in life.

Due to extreme sensitivity, there may be nervous irritability and at times, meaningless chatter which compensates for general insecurity and shyness. They are sentimental but their personalities are extremely changeable, ranging from extreme warmth to secrecy, which is often mistaken for coldness. Cancerians feel safe and secure surrounded by family and the comforts of home, though they sometimes go through their entire lives searching for it. With difficult aspects, they can be quick-tempered, irritable and dishonest. Cancerians have great ups and downs in money matters, unless they have conquered their speculative tendency early in life.

People born in this sign often reach exalted positions or gain some pinnacle of fame where they cannot escape the dazzling lights of publicity. In fact they are dreamers of large plans. They evolve big ideas for the welfare of others, but if they meet opposition and criticism they suffer silently and are inclined to be pessimistic.

Cancer, like the ocean tides which it governs, is changeable and fluctuating. These qualities will manifest in their life as moods which are up one day and down the next. They must be careful that this moodiness does not develop into extremist tendencies. They must try to maintain an even balance and remember that moderation in all they do is best.

This ability links up with Cancer's affinity with Water, which will always adapt itself to the shape of the container which holds it.

They are sympathetic towards people in distress and it is remarkable how many times Cancer on the ascendant brings contact with suffering and troubles of others. Perhaps this is because they have some of the martyr in their nature.

They like the security of a home base because their home, domestic and family life is of prime importance. A career or other interests are all very well but they need home life to achieve complete fulfillment. Cancer is the sign of home lovers and homemakers.

CANCER (MOON SIGN)

KARK (He, Hu, He, Ho, D, Da, Di, De, Do)

The highly developed Cancer is a master of many moods, forever constant in his inconsistency. He can make others feel joy, sorrow, horror and compassion. He is endowed with immense sensitivity and his vivid imagination can take hold of any emotion and morbid feelings. There is a yearning for short trips and travel. However, the native shall always come back to his home which he holds most dear. The native's mental powers are strong. His scrupulous and open temperament make him vulnerable to deceit. It endows him with a strong mind and body.

Dramatic by nature, he enjoys an audience which ensures definite growth. However there may be unforeseen hindrances – tiredness and tension – but finally his ambition takes an unusual form in career.

The Cancerian will have some violent deed committed against him and he shall be surrounded by problems, but assistance and relief will come to him from a female, usually the mother or spouse.

In disposition he is changeable, fickle, fond of travel and novelty, although he does not dislike his domestic circle and his family, to whom he is greatly attached, until the day comes when he realises that his feelings are not reciprocated. He will then escape without hope of ever returning.

He is sociable, intellectual, poetical, inclined to be pessimistic and to worry about the future, and this will make him economical. Cancer is a lucky sign. It often enables the native to make a rich marriage and gain several inheritances. For a man, it often brings wealth through women.

CANCER – YOUR PERSONAL OUTLOOK

The Cancer-born has a middle-sized plump body. He is intelligent, industrious and proud. He is honest, talkative, independent and sensitive, but also miserly. He has a number of good friends, but few children. The spouse will be well-mannered and devoted.

Following are the general characteristics:

- Medium stature
- Delicate bones
- Plump and well-rounded body
- Small hands and feet
- Bluish or gray eyes

CANCER – YOUR OCCULT FOUNDATION

Cancer's rulling planet is Moon, whose occult value is two. Two has passive, feminine properties. Its duality is symbolised by horns, which have association with the crescent Moon and with mother goddess. Thus on a positive note, two embraces her attributes. Goddess is primarily a symbol of fertility, she who brings forth all life, which cannot prosper without her blessing. In mythology, she appears often in a triple aspect representing maiden, mother and crone, with such aspects as youth, adulthood and old age, and virgin, nurturer and destroyer. In her many roles, goddess rules over wisdom, truth, magical powers, nature, fate, home, healing, justice, love, birth, death, time and eternity. She also rules the inner self – one's emotion, intuition, psychic forces and mysteries.

Two also represents ignorance, but even this cloud has a silver lining, for out of ignorance emerges wisdom. Two is the darkness before the light. In mythology, two often signifies the emergence of something into the consciousness.

In Christian symbolism, two represents the dual nature of Christ (good and human). In Kabbalistic symbolism it represents wisdom and self-consciousness.

FINANCE AND PROFESSION

Though Cancer is a money-making sign, insecurity will always come their way. Changeable conditions will also apply. There is likely to be a general feeling of uncertainty, giving way to a desire to jump at any chance to make money. This is likely in the end to become a kind of vicious circle, which is inclined to become worse as one gets older.

Extreme caution should be exercised while dealing in financial matters. They should avoid speculation and all forms of gambling. They should endeavour to build up their reserves, no matter how slowly. All, get rich quick" schemes should be avoided and if possible they should become associated with or work for solid established businesses.

Their planetary conditions favour shipping, exports and transportation of goods or people, or the opening up of undeveloped countries.

Cancerians have commercial careers. Maybe as a sailor in the navy, shipping, import and export, transport or travel. They can also be a restaurant manager, orator, preacher, or contractor. They are interested in developing Vedic and sacred texts.

HEALTH AND FOOD

They will be extremely sensitive to their surroundings; if these are fortunate they will probably get through life without much trouble. If, on the contrary, they are forced to live under depressing or unhappy conditions, they will be liable to suffer a great deal from physical illness. In other words, with a Cancerian, it will be largely a question of the effect of 'mind over matter'. The general tendency will be for almost unaccountable pains and internal cramps in the internal organs. There will be some likelihood of tumours, lesions in connection with the intestines.

The following food should be included in their diet:

- Fish
- Potatoes
- Water melon
- Melon
- Mushroom

They should avoid pastries, cakes and junk food.

CANCER AS A LOVER

Male

Life without romance is monotonous to this lover, yet he is loyal, sincere and affectionate in love, but undemonstrative in loyalty and sincerity. Once involved, he is a sincere and ardent lover. Romantic and passionate, he is difficult to understand, and is sensitive and secretive.

He is compatible with

Taurus:	Romance, marriage, business and lasting friendship.
Cancer:	A sensitive relationship but good for friendship and sex.
Scorpio:	Romance, marriage, business and lasting friendship.
Pisces:	Sex, Love and marriage.

He is incompatible with

Aries
Gemini
Virgo
Libra

Female

She is sincere, loyal and devoted, but becomes moody at times. When neglected, overlooked or ignored, she becomes stubborn, determined and unyielding and may change her partner as she cannot tolerate this.

She is compatible with

Taurus:	Romance, marriage, business and lasting friendship.
Pisces:	Sex, love and marriage.

She is incompatible with

Leo
Libra
Sagittarius

YOUR RELATIONSHIPS

Cancer with Cancer

The emotional nature is related to their element of Water, so two Cancerians will produce a relationship in which feelings and emotions play a dominant role. If both agree, this combination will bring great happiness, but the reverse also can apply. Both are sympathetic and compassionate, so they will help the other in times of trouble. Emotions can sometimes make clear thinking difficult, or some upsetting or muddled situation can occur when things go wrong.

Astro Advice

- The man should carry roses or white lilies to cherish his beloved.
- The woman should be practical and reliable. She should not be over-sentimental.

Cancer with Leo

Although Water is not compatible with Fire, their respective rulers, the Moon and the Sun, complement each other. So, in spite of their different natures, there will be a strong bond. Cancer often will have to give way to dominant Leo, but Leo has qualities which make a Cancer's Moon shine more brightly. Leo needs appreciation and attention, which Cancer is happy to give.

Astro Advice

- The man should spend money wisely on his beloved.
- The woman should learn to be cheerful while going to meet her beloved.

Cancer with Virgo

Water, which is compatible with Earth, enhances the merits of this combination. Cancer proves sincere, loyal and conscientious and so will appreciate the hallmarks of Virgo which are care, attention to detail and thoroughness. Cancer is patient and, therefore, willing to accept. Virgo will not be happy with quick but shoddy work. Virgo is too much of a perfectionist to do things in a hurry. Cancer is hypersensitive and easily hurt, so Virgo should curb the tendency to criticise when Cancer errs. Cancer should remember that Virgo is not too demonstrative when it comes to expressing feelings of love or affection.

Astro Advice

- The woman should dress up in traditional wear with a red bindi on her forehead.
- The man should wear pearl of five rattis on Monday after Pran Pratishta (prayer to Moon).

Cancer with Libra

Although Water and Air are not very compatible, their respective rulers – Moon and Venus – have much in common and they harmonise. Cancer is easily hurt but, unless peace-loving Libra is provoked, it is unlikely to do anything to cause conflict deliberately. Libra will appreciate Cancer's natural desire to love and protection, but sometimes will impose on the Cancerian's desire to give. Libra likes a balance between emotion and reason, so may be disturbed on occasions by Cancer's excess of emotion.

Astro Advice

- The man should wear white stone of seven rattis on Friday after Pran Pratishta (prayer to Venus).
- The woman should wear pearl of five rattis on Monday after Pran Pratishta (prayer to Moon).

Cancer with Scorpio

Water with Water is compatible but, since this element is related to feelings and emotions, rather than facts and logic, these will predominate. When harmony reigns, this is a constructive duo but, if conflicts arise, emotions go out of control and distort clear thinking. Each one is intuitive and can sense what is going on, so mutual trust is essential. Cancer has his own way of understanding that Scorpio can be tough and ruthless.

Astro Advice

- Both should understand each others' feelings.
- The woman should be confident while speaking.

Cancer with Sagittarius

This combination of Water with Fire highlights the great differences in their natures. Without good communication they could feel that they live in different worlds, because Sagittarius is far too wayward and freedom-loving to be domesticated and home-oriented like Cancer. Sagittarius is mentally, emotionally and physically independent, which can make Cancer feel insecure. Both are generous, in different ways. Cancer is inclined to cling, which can cause Sagittarius to feel smothered or trapped.

Astro Advice

- The woman should wear yellow sapphire of five rattis on Thursday after Pran Pratishta (prayer to Jupiter).
- The man should wear pearl of seven rattis on Monday after Pran Pratishta (prayer to Moon).

Cancer with Capricorn

Water is compatible with Earth, but because these are opposite signs in the zodiac, the combination can not only be complementary, but also competitive. If Capricorn gives top priority to ambition and success, sensitive Cancer will feel hurt or neglected. The Moon child admires and benefits from Capricorn's sense of duty and responsibility but Capricorn sometimes lacks the sentiment, warmth and loving care which is so important to Cancer.

Astro Advice

- The man should wear blue sapphire of six rattis on Saturday after Pran Pratishta (prayer to Saturn).

- The woman should try to sort out differences of opinion.

Cancer with Aquarius

Long periods together will soon reveal that their respective rulers – the Watery Moon and Airy Saturn have little in common. Cancer's sensitive feelings and clinging emotions can disturb Aquarius, who needs time for independent and detached action. In a way, Aquarius is a universal, rather than a personal lover, who likes to share interests and affections with friends and humanity.

Astro Advice

- The man should not be in the grip of false hopes.
- The woman needs to take care of her body and health.

Cancer with Pisces

This unites two Water signs and since the Water element is related to feelings, emotions and intuition, these will always have priority over logic, reasoning and analysis. In this combination of signs some practical necessities can become muddled or confused. Both feel deeply, so each can evoke a sympathetic response in the other even without a word being spoken. Both are very romantic and need to love and be loved.

Astro Advice

- The man should not forget to carry a pack of chocolates with him.

- The woman should remember her beloved believes in Spartan simplicity.

ASTRO GUIDE

How to improve your luck

Lucky Date:	2nd, 11th, 20th, 29th, of any month
Lucky Day:	Monday for meetings, Saturday for love and romance.
Lucky Colour:	White, light yellow, sea colour. These should be used as curtains, bed sheets and as colour of wall. Attire should also match lucky colour.
Lucky Gem:	Pearl or cat's eye.
Lucky Metal:	Silver, aluminium and platinum.
Lucky Flower:	White rose, jasmine.
Mantra:	Aum Shran Shrin Shron Sei: Chandraye Namah.
Lucky Talisman:	Shoe in silver to be worn next to skin.

LEO

THE LION

(23rd July – 23rd August)
The Sign of the King or President

- Governs the heart and upper part of the spine.
- Planetary Ruler: Sun.
- Virtues: Ambitious, energetic, authoritative.
- Vices: Dogmatic, argumentative, arrogant.

LEO (SUN SIGN)

Represented by the Lion, king of the jungle, Leos must be in control of their lives at all times. They do not like working for others and everything they do must have their personal stamp. But Leo can also represent one of the most generous and magnanimous signs of the zodiac, capable of being wonderful hosts and hostesses.

Persons born during this period are extremely sympathetic, generous, honest, straightforward and authoritative. They are proud and lucky in money matters. They possess a strong will-power and great tenacity of purpose. They usually achieve their objectives in spite of difficulties or obstacles. The careers best suited to them are the armed forces, civil services, finance, business and politics. In matters of love, they are possessive, passionate and loyal. They crave for love, which often eludes them due to their stubborn temperament.

In addition to being constructive and inventive, Leos are good organisers, directors and 'ideas men', who leave the detailed and technical work to others. They enjoy being admired and praised for their accomplishments and desperately need the approval of others. Difficult aspects make them too demanding, too authoritative and too egoistic to concern themselves with the needs and opinions of others.

People born in this period are large-hearted and generous. They have an extremely independent spirit, they detest control or being dictated to. They have much tenacity of purpose and will-power and if they put their mind on some plan, purpose or position, they usually reach their goal in spite of every difficulty or obstacle.

They have a wonderful magnetic power in inspiring others to do great deeds.

They make enemies by their frankness of speech and their hatred of anything underhand. They will defend a friend in the face of all attacks and it is only treachery, disloyalty or deceit that can ever break or crush their proud spirit.

They radiate warmth, affection, kindness and a strong personal magnetism, which makes them exceedingly popular. Highly susceptible to environment, they exhibit a strong tendency to take on the habits and conditions of others. However a Leo cannot be overlooked in a crowd. He is well proportionate; his regal bearing and high laughter will frequently resemble a roar. Discordant and numinous environments can effect his health. His best medicine is peace, love, warmth and harmony.

LEO (MOON SIGN)

SINH (M, Me, Mu, Mo, T, Ta, Te, To, Tu)

Leo's regal bearing and good appearance give authoritative disposition, which endows and blesses him with the very best in life. Success and growth is certain in a professional or academic line. It creates the writer, scientist, the musician, the poet. It showers determination, aspirations and hardwork. Temperament is blunt, egoistic and vain. The sign symbolises a person of sound advice who can assist other people.

Since energy and vitality is high, the native may at times take on more than he can handle. He shall be able to prosper by virtue of his hard work and determination.

Placed in Leo, the Moon can cause poor vision and force the native to start wearing spectacles at an early period in life.

It signifies fidelity and an inclination to be overly trusting of one and all.

The native goes straight ahead, his confidence in his strength and success enabling him to take a pleasant view of life. He is full of vitality. Capable of great exertion, and knowing exactly what he wants, he succeeds along his chosen path, provided that the lord of this sign, the Sun, is well situated.

Leo in the ascendant often means two marriages, denoting separation for the native or his parents. This prevents the period of youth from being exactly what he would like it to be. He will nevertheless attain a higher position than his father.

LEO – YOUR PERSONAL OUTLOOK

The Leo-born is tall, bold, generous and respectable. He has broad shoulders and is inclined to quick anger. Success comes to him only after much struggle. He will remain devoted to his parents.

They will have the following characteristics:

- Average stature
- Clear complexion
- Full and round face
- Muscles

LEO – YOUR OCCULT FOUNDATION

Leo is ruled by the Sun, whose occult value is number one. The Pythagoreans called one the monad and equated it with God, the beginning and end of all things and the source. One is the mystic centre. It is the spiritual unity that unites all beings. It is mind, which gives it stability, for mind is stable. Unlike other odd numbers, one is most masculine, but is hermaphroditic in nature, comprising both male and female principles, because one added to an even number makes an odd number, and added to an odd number makes an even one. From one issues all other numbers; no number can exist without it.

The Pythagoreans associated one with the names of various deities, whose attributes reflected the qualities of one.

Symbols related to one include the ship and the chariot. One points to beginings, creation, unity, divinity, light and matters of spirit and mind. It is an auspicious number, holding promise and optimism.

FINANCE AND PROFESSION

They have full potential and capability in making money. They may have to meet hardship and difficulties in early years, but will forge ahead out of any unfavourable conditions and will have every prospect of becoming well off and will gain power and position wherever they may be.

Their career will be divided as it were into the zones. Up to about thirty-seven years, they will have to do plenty of hard work in overcoming difficulties, from thirty-seven to the end they will enjoy a more or less prosperous and successful life. Leo is the sign of successful profession relating to taxes. They are also painters, jewellers, astrologers, sportsmen and more generally connected with high quality work. They are enthusiastic and careful about money.

Leos can be the best educators, politicians, occupy high positions in the government; they have executive ability and are managers of big concerns and corporations, directors, captains, sales managers, etc.

HEALTH AND FOOD

In their childhood and early years, they will be liable to many minor illnesses, especially fevers, rheumatism, inflammation of the blood, carbuncles, boils, etc. But as they become older they will grow out of such problems and become healthy and vigorous.

The heart and many times the eyes are weak health areas. The nerves and reserves of energy should not be taxed. Sometimes the solar plexus can malfunction.

The following food should be included in their diet:

- Lemons
- Coconut
- Litchi
- Honey
- Green vegetables

They should avoid red meat.

LEO AS A LOVER

Male

He is an ideal lover – romantic, fiery in passion but sincere and faithful in love. To show love publicly is below his dignity. He is good-hearted, fond of the opposite sex and remains surrounded by ladies. It is safe to have commitments once his heart has been won.

He is compatible with:

Aries:	Love, marriage, business partnership.
Gemini:	Romance, sex, marriage, business and long lasting friendship.
Sagittarius:	Romance, marriage, business and lasting friendship.
Pisces:	Physically an excellent union.

He is incompatible with:

Taurus
Cancer
Virgo
Libra
Aquarius

Female

She is ambitious and ideal and should not doubt her lovers. She has everlasting love, but needs to be kept under control. Popular with the opposite sex and not selfish, she is very passionate and requires self-control lest she goes beyond limits. She is of fixed ideas, dogmatic views and expects her word to be law.

She is compatible with:

Leo:	Romance, marriage, business and lasting friendship.
Libra:	Physically, an excellent union.

She is incompatible with:

Scorpio
Capricorn

YOUR RELATIONSHIPS

Leo with Leo

Fire with Fire in two such positive, strong-willed people can be either good or bad. Two Leos constitute all the membership required for a mutual admiration society. As a team they offer no less than they offer the rest of the Sun signs. Capable of heroic sacrifice and hardships in the name of love or friendship, these two also fight, shout and make up more often than any other combinations. But these proud people can usually harmonise their differences.

Astro Advice

- The man should wear ruby of six rattis on Sunday after Pran Pratishta (prayer to Sun).
- The woman should wear white stone of five rattis on Monday after Pran Pratishta (prayer to Venus).

Leo with Virgo

Fire with Earth in two such positive strong-willed people can be either good or bad. Mutual give and take will be necessary to make this combination work. Alternatively, one will have to play second fiddle, but which one? There is nothing they cannot do if their goals and methods happen to agree.

Astro Advice

- The man should give proper to attention to his beloved.
- The woman should wear emerald of six rattis on Wednesday.

Leo with Libra

Fire is compatible with Air and, since both have a natural ability for enjoying the same good things in life, they will share lots of happy times. Libra, who likes to keep things balanced, may think that Leo is too extravagant, generous, flamboyant or lavish.

There is a lot of communication at various levels between Leos and Librans. Friendships of the genuine kind are more common among these two. Life presents them with an unending stream of opportunities in every area and when they join forces, they can achieve almost anything! Leos just have to figure out by 'discussion', Librans do not mean dramatic scenes or angry outbursts.

Astro Advice

- The man should not lack motivation, ambition, or drive to face challenges.
- The woman should sense the potential and look forward to what lies ahead.

Leo with Scorpio

Fire with Water in two such powerful, strong-willed signs can prove a stormy combination unless neither tries to control or dominate the other. There is almost no limit to what this team can achieve if their goals coincide and they strive together. Leo, frank and open, will not understand Scorpio's secret, subtle manoeuvres and the Sun child often will disapprove of them.

Astro Advice

- The man should wear pearl of six rattis on Monday.
- The woman should avoid being stubborn.

Leo with Sagittarius

This combination of Fire with Fire will work well because their respective rulers – the Sun and Jupiter – are positive, optimistic and take a broad viewpoint. Since both are frank, generous and open-hearted, they can enrich each other. Independent Sagittarius will rebel if Leo tries to boss or control. The little Lion will fret or feel neglected if Sagittarius is too eager for freedom.

Astro Advice

- The man should be warm and soft in his behaviour.
- The woman should carry a bunch of flowers while going to meet her beloved.

Leo with Capricorn

Fire with Earth highlights the great difference between these two signs and their respective rulers – the brilliant, grandiose Sun and conservative, austere Saturn. In a prolonged, close relationship, Leo would feel too hemmed in or restricted by Capricorn, who in turn, will feel that Leo's ways are too extravagant or demonstrative to be warranted. Leo likes to live life to the full whereas Capricorn, being more cautious and conservative, likes to plan for the future. Capricorn is emotionally reserved and fairly undemonstrative and seldom realises that Leo can feel starved unless given lots of love, affection, attention and appreciation.

Astro Advice

- The man should wear blue sapphire of six rattis on Saturday after Pran Pratishta (prayer to Saturn).

- The woman should wear ruby of six rattis on Sunday after Pran Pratishta (prayer to Sun).

Leo with Aquarius

Although Fire has a natural affinity with Air, these signs are opposite each other in the zodiac. There can be a strong initial attraction which sometimes is transformed into equally strong opposition. They both have fixed opinions, strong determination and minds of their own; so, without compromise, there will be a clash of wills. Leo will feel justified in claiming most of the partner's attention, so will find it difficult to accept the fact that Aquarius likes to share interests, activities, ideals and affection with more than one person. Leo will not understand why Aquarius should be so unpredictable, detached at the most unexpected times.

Astro Advice

- Both should avoid getting caught in controversial issues.

Leo with Pisces

Fire with Water highlights the great difference between these two. Leo is one of the most frank, open, extrovert signs. Pisces has deep, mysterious, elusive qualities which are almost unfathomable to most people. Leo never really knows what Pisces is made of, but the latter admires the strengthened purpose of Leo. Pisces often needs to be more organised and Leo is just the one to do it.

Astro Advice

- The man should show his feeling by giving gifts and cards.
- The woman should wear yellow sapphire of six carats on the index finger.

ASTRO GUIDE

How to improve your luck

Lucky Date: All series of 1 and 4, 10th, 19th, 13th, 22nd, 31st.

Lucky Day: Sunday for meetings, Friday for love and romance.

Lucky Colour: Red, orange and white. These should be used as curtains, bed sheets and as colour of wall. Attire should also match lucky colour.

Lucky Gem: Ruby or amber of five rattis to be worn on the ring finger on Sunday morning after Pran Pratishtha.

Lucky Flower: Red rose, sunflower, rosemary.

Mantra: Aum Hran Hrin Hron Sei: Suryaye Namah.

Lucky Talisman: Sun in gold to be worn next to skin.

VIRGO

THE VIRGIN

(24th August – 23rd September)
The Sign of the Craftsman or Critic

- Governs the abdominal region.
- Planetary Ruler: Mercury.
- Virtues: Exact, methodical, discriminating.
- Vices: Oversensitive, sarcastic, chatty.

VIRGO (SUN SIGN)

As the sign of the Virgin, Virgos search for purity through cleanliness, good health, proper diet and exercise. They are sensitive, reserved, self-conscious, critical and fastidious. As they are ruled by inconstant Mercury, Virgos are prone to change, whether it be residences, jobs or points of view.

Persons born during this period are generally successful in life. They possess good judgments and keen analytical power. They are neither easily impressed nor deceived by others. They always try to maintain a high standard of living. Virgos can be successful in business, and are also capable of adapting themselves to numerous vocations such as banking, medicine, journalism, law and telecommunications. On the emotional front however, they are difficult to understand. Both strong and weak characters are found in this Sun Sign.

They are conscientious and methodical workers capable of functioning under any adversity and also make excellent organisers. Virgos can be very insecure and reserved, qualities which may be interpreted as lack of warmth and goodwill. Because they are perfectionists, they are often dissatisfied and too critical of themselves as well as others.

With difficult aspects, Virgos tend to have a pessimistic outlook on life spending too much time analysing and worrying which may adversely affect their health.

They are modest and conservative and they do not particularly like the limelight, especially when it brings them into close contact with other people. One noticeable feature which they derive from the position of Virgo on the ascendant is a dislike of being touched by other people. This somewhat virgin-like quality makes them almost indifferent to physical passion and violent emotions and probably accounts for the fact that quite a high percentage of people who are born with Virgo on the ascendant prefer to remain single.

If the negative side of Virgo is allowed to develop, their critical and discriminative faculties will degenerate into constant display of nagging and fault-finding. Their emphasis on detail also must be kept well under control because it can easily develop into over-fastidiousness. Virgo is much more interested in mental accomplishment than in physical prowess but it is important to go for Yoga, meditation and physical exercise.

They are not as a rule originators, but they carry out with success any plan or work that appeals to them, or things which others have failed to finish.

They have unusual respect for rank and position; they are jealous supporters of the law and the law's decision. They make excellent lawyers and debaters, but they tend to support precedents more than originating any new ordinance. They are inclined to become wrapped up in themselves and their own ideas; they appear to become selfish in the close pursuit of their aims. They are generally self-possessed and self-reliant.

They are extremely sensitive to their surroundings, the least disharmony or annoyance affects their nervous system and upsets their digestive organs.

VIRGO (MOON SIGN)

KANYA (To, Pa, Pe, Pu, Sh, Na, Th, Pe, Po)

Virgo (Kanya), the symbol of the Virgin, is signified by a discriminating nature. It gives the native an odd temperament. His mind shall be highly perceptive and this will allow him to prosper in the occult world. It will give him an inclination towards dreams, second sight, enlightenment. He will commit errors as a result of lack of logic and experience. If adversely aspected by Mars, he shall not be hard-working.

If born during the early hours, the wicked effect of Saturn will result in severe digestive ailments. This situation causes the gravest stomach problems in females, often making them barren. Despite the disorders, the Moon endows the native with a long life. Marriage, however, is based more on emotions than fortune.

If born in midday it is unfortunate from the materialistic viewpoint. It will always result in postponement of the native's plans and their implementation and he may do things which shall fail, since he will lack a solid base.

The native's mental aptitude is good, but often not employed to the best advantage. In spite of organisation in details, there is a lack of ideas from the synthetic standpoint, so that, unless Mars, Uranus or Saturn are powerful in the horoscope, the native will have more chance to succeed with others than alone.

It is a good position for taking up science, medicine or occultism and also gives great adaptability for commercial pursuits.

The native gives freely of his time and energy, but nevertheless there is a limit to his generosity. Love never comes easily to him, it takes much to melt his heart, but once committed he remains faithful and loyal to his partner.

VIRGO – YOUR PERSONAL OUTLOOK

Virgos have a sharp intellect and a slender, middle-sized stature. They are impulsive, religious and influential. They are fond of learning and may be interested in art, literature, or science. They are usually shy. Spouse will be good-looking and devoted.

They will have the following characteristics:

- Slim body
- Round face and forehead
- Sallow complexion
- Hair colour matching the eyes

VIRGO – YOUR OCCULT FOUNDATION

Virgo is ruled by Mercury, whose occult value is five, which is essentially the microcosm. This number symbolises the physical man and his five senses and thus connotes sensuality and pleasure. It also resonates with higher qualities; it is man with his four limbs plus a head, the four cardinal points with the centre, the four elements plus a fifth element of ether, the universal vitalising substance that permeates all things. In this respect, five is the number of hierophant. Since five divides the perfect number 10, equally into two parts, it represents equilibrium and balance.

FINANCE AND PROFESSION

They are so versatile that it would almost be impossible, to pick out any one career in which they would be best in making money. They can fit in any position and make money in almost anything.

They are bound at times to have 'strokes of good luck', but as a rule they cannot put money aside for the advanced years. When they have a run of good fortune they should buy an annuity so as to protect themselves against their own lack of provision for the future. They can be successful as professionals and accumulate lot of wealth, but a lack of responsibility can almost crush them. However, they spend the money wisely and well.

Virgos are slaves to work, hard taskmasters and like to be left alone. They are fit for becoming brokers, accountants, lawyers, journalists, engineers, surgeons and professionals connected with liquid, etc.

HEALTH AND FOOD

They live too much on their nerves. They are generally tense most of the time and in consequence are subject to nervous break-downs.

They often have a twitching in some part of the face, a slight stammering in speech, trouble with the nerves of the tongue and a tendency in advanced years towards paralysis or cramp of the lower limbs. As a rule they will be light sleepers or suffer from insomnia and not get enough rest and sleep.

An environment which is not harmonious generally affects their lifestyle. They should eat well and do some light exercises. The lungs, bowels, hips and feet come under troubled areas.

The following food should be included in their diet:

- Lemon
- Almonds
- Grains
- Cheese
- Lamb

VIRGO AS A LOVER

Male

He gives more weight to intelligence than pleasure and romance. He will insist on knowing the sincerity of the partner's feelings. He is a loyal lover with a very romantic nature. This is only revealed to the person he loves. So courtship can be full of surprises.

He is compatible with:

Capricorn: Romance, sex, marriage, business and long lasting friendship.

Pisces: Sex and great friendship.

He is incompatible with:

Aries
Gemini
Libra
Sagittarius

Female

She is intelligent, wise, of accommodating nature and considers sex to be troublesome, but if advised can be an excellent sex companion. She admires others as she wants appreciation. Shy, but not demonstrative in love. Passionate but has a fault-finding nature.

She is compatible with:

Taurus: Romance, sex, marriage, business and long lasting friendship.

Virgo: A great friendship, sex.

Scorpio: A good relationship.

Capricorn: Romance, sex, marriage, business and long lasting friendship.

Pisces: Sex and great friendship.

She is incompatible with:

Aries
Cancer
Leo

YOUR RELATIONSHIPS

Virgo with Virgo

Earth is compatible with Earth, but it does not double up on practical, down-to-earth, realistic qualities of their sign. Because of this fact, each likes to have an organised routine and it is easy to fall into a rut. Neither will make impossible emotional demands on the other, but each should avoid nagging or fault-finding .

Astro Advice

- The man should wear emerald of six rattis on Wednesday.
- The woman should wear diamond of one carat on Friday.

Virgo with Libra

Virgos are gentle and courteous by nature; Librans are sharp and swift. Virgo is a quiet, peaceful soul who will accept Libra's logic, long discussions and cheerful optimism for a long time. They will blissfully wander and will not raise their voices in shouting and all will be melodious and marvellous. Virgo will cheerfully and willingly accept restrictions, disappointments and will sacrifice a lot for his/her beloved. And Libra with his/her Venus fairness and justice respects and reciprocates feelings with love and free spirit. Depression causes more pain in Libra than any other person and he/she can be very lonely.

Astro Advice

- The man should understand that his beloved needs emotional security.
- The woman should try to be honest and straightforward.

Virgo with Scorpio

In practical and intellectual areas, this combination of Earth with Water will work well. But emotionally these two signs are worlds apart. Scorpio has intense feelings and burning desires; whereas Virgo believes in controlling them. Sexually, both require adjustments and gradually it can be an experience of mutual passion. Both are friends and lovers to the extent that even violent disagreements can be the beginning of a new relationship.

Astro Advice

- The woman should wear any sort of headgear as it would be eye-catching.
- The man should wear grey clothes and the neckline should have a 'V' shape.

Virgo with Sagittarius

Earthy Virgo is careful, methodical, controlled and analytical. Fiery Sagittarius is impulsive, quick, independent and sometimes reckless or extravagant. Virgo is mentally equipped and specialised to concentrate on one thing at a time and can also handle small details and live in the present. Sagittarius is broad-minded, optimistic and always looks to the future. Self-expression of both these signs flows through very different channels.

Astro Advice

- The man should wear yellow sapphire of eight rattis on Thursday.
- The woman should wear emerald of five rattis on Wednesday.

Virgo with Capricorn

These signs belong to the element Earth, so they both have their feet on the ground and appreciate the practical side of life and work. Both are conscientious, with a strong sense of duty and responsibility, but they should avoid a pattern of 'all work and no play'. Their respective rulers, intellectual Mercury and self-disciplined Saturn, are well-matched for business and practical matters, but there could be a lack of feelings, warm emotions and romantic sparkle. Capricorn admires the systematic, methodical, well-ordered ways of Virgo, while the latter is sufficiently self-contained and logical.

Astro Advice

- The man should not be materialistic.
- The woman should curb overspending.

Virgo with Aquarius

Earth with Air highlights the contrast between these two signs. The combination of their respective rulers – Mercury and Uranus – emphasises a mental and intellectual affinity, rather than a deep emotional bond. Virgo is sensible, rational, analytical and sometimes cool, while Aquarius can be dispassionate, detached, uninvolved. Virgo is careful, self-controlled and orthodox, but Aquarius can be unpredictable, temperamental and unconventional at times. Virgo's logical mind cannot begin to decipher the enigma that is in Aquarius.

Astro Advice

- The man should show his feelings by giving gifts and flowers.
- The woman should wear a gold bangle or bracelet.

Virgo with Pisces

Earth has an affinity with Water and these opposite signs in the zodiac can complement each other. Virgo is motivated by reason, analysis, facts and logic, whereas Pisces is guided by feelings, emotions, intuitions and that strange ability to sense what others feel. Both can add a touch of magic to each other's life.

Astro Advice

- The woman should realise that lying can create problems.
- The man should wear emerald of eight rattis on Wednesday.

ASTRO GUIDE

How to improve your luck

Lucky Date: All series of 5 and 14th, 23rd.

Lucky Day: Wednesday for meetings, Friday for love and romance.

Lucky Colour: Green and white; these should be used as curtains, bed sheets and as colour of wall. Attire should also match lucky colour.

Lucky Gem: Emerald to be worn on Wednesday morning on the little finger after pran pratishtha.

Lucky Metal: Gold and silver.

Lucky Flower: Flowers which are light yellow in colour.

Mantra: Aum Bran Brin Bron Se: Bhodhaye Namah.

Lucky Talisman: Key or serpent in gold to be worn next to skin.

LIBRA

THE SCALES

(24th September – 23rd October)
The Sign of the Statesman or Manager

- Governs the kidneys and lower part of the back.
- Planetary Ruler: Venus.
- Virtues: Harmonious, graceful, beautiful, kind.
- Vices: Indecisive, escapist, vain.

LIBRA (SUN SIGN)

The symbol of a pair of Scales of justice indicates love of balance and harmony. Venus is the ruling planet, so they are gentle, soft-spoken, modest and courteous. Persons born during this period are decisive in their thoughts and actions. They have great foresight and intuition. They are diplomatic, alert, balanced and just. They have a large circle of friends and acquaintances. All sorts of careers are suitable to them, though they are more successful as lawyers, judges, politicians, diplomats and salespersons. They often hold a prominent position in public life. On the marital front, however, they are seldom happy.

They have a difficult time making decisions and can be lazy, excessive with drugs and alcohol, especially in case of an unsuccessful love affair. There is too much concern with appearances, attire and they often adjust their personalities to suit their partner. Love life is of permanent importance in their life, even in old age they rarely lose interest.

Librans are very often fond of public life, but they generally go in for it from the standpoint of their desire to adjust for the betterment of their fellow beings.

Just as the balance can tip easily from one side of the scale to other, so they can be changeable both in ideas and moods. They may be giving all of their attention to a particular hobby or line of thought and then, almost without warning, drop it. They have a strong sense of justice and will never allow a wrong to go uncorrected. They are pleasant, with a charming disposition, and to be happy they must have peace and harmony around them. In fact, peace at any price could well be the motto of Librans.

Librans are naturally artistic, with a good eye for design, so their home will always be tactfully decorated. Beauty and elegance are important and they will spare no expenses when buying anything which accentuates these qualities.

They are affectionate and make friends easily, so their social life is not only likely to be interesting but also profitable, providing opportunities for furthering their success. As they have an intense dislike of conflict, tension and discord, most people find it easy to get along with them.

Many born in this sign spend a lifetime in study or research work of some particular kind; some make excellent scientists and doctors who pursue a special line of study, but whatever they do, they generally do thoroughly. They have a multifaceted nature and have numerous moods, to which they give a great variety of expression. They have little or no regard for the value of money and rarely involve themselves in rash speculation and reckless enterprise.

LIBRA (MOON SIGN)

TULA (Ra, Ri, Ru, Re, Ro, Ta, Te, Tu, T)

Libra (Tula) symbolised by Scales, is intelligent, talkative and versatile. Dishonesty and melancholy are not his characteristics. They go through life attempting to establish a beautiful and harmonious environment for those with whom he comes into contact.

The native has a direct and dutiful mind, but is slightly reticent. Everything about him is dignified and cultured, including his attire, which exudes austerity. Happiness and an ever-present wish for recreation will prompt Librans to enjoy the company of people younger than them.

Logic and pragmatism characterise the Libra native and his clear and fertile imagination make him a fluent speaker – one who does not diverge from the main topic.

When born during sunrise, Librans usually become successful political or judicial figures and are noted for their keen sense of justice and fairness.

Libra gives fine intellectual qualities and a certain degree of ambition especially in a feminine horoscope. The character is even, kindly, gentle, well-balanced, artistic and the native will succeed without great difficulty.

This position indicates early marriage. Libra does not usually give great physical courage, as the native can obtain what he wants without much exertion.

If born at the time of sunset, vocation or career may cause some anxiety, for they may make a wrong decision or take a wrong turn in terms of friendship, union, business or marriage.

LIBRA – YOUR PERSONAL OUTLOOK

The Libra-born is lean and of middle height. They are clever at making schemes as they possess a sound judgement. They are popular, and lovers of art. By nature they are practical. Spouse will be of quarrelsome nature.

A Libran will have the following characteristics:

- Rounded and comely face
- Pink and white complexion
- Chestnut or light hair
- Bright and compelling eyes
- Long and silky lashes

LIBRA – YOUR OCCULT FOUNDATION

Libra is ruled by Venus, whose occult value is six. The number of equilibrium, as well as balance, harmony, health and time. The six-sided figure, the hexagon is formed by the union of two triangles. In addition, this union represents marriage and the hermaphrodite, both of which are the result of the union of the male and female. The Pythagoreans considered six the form of forms, the perfection of all the parts, and associated it with immortality. In Christian symbolism, six is also the number of perfection because God created the world in six days. In Kabbalism, six represents beauty and creation. In shapes, six is represented by the hexagram, the symbol of the union of opposites.

FINANCE AND PROFESSION

They will be fortunate in investments and in finance generally, especially if they follow their own intuition. They will be lucky in partnership, business investments or in matters dealing with the public. They vacillate too much and can face problems in finding a right profession where they can make money. The Libran should be firm and positive and be ready to say 'No.' This could lead them to a positive situation in business.

Could be a government servant or officer. Will lead a public social life. Best suited for law, chemist, liquid items, electrical engineers, transport, navy, painters, etc. They could also be dealing with articles of feminine interests and luxury or amusement items. Can be writer, musician, singer or actor.

HEALTH AND FOOD

On account of their having great recuperative power, they are not likely to have health problems with the exception of having easily bruised flesh from which there may be some danger of tumours. In the early years they are likely to have inflamed tonsils and some trouble at the back of the tongue and throat. The kidney, the back, the buttocks, generative organs are weak health zones. The nervous system is sensitive. Ugly environment and disturbed atmosphere could result in ill-health.

They following food should be included in their diet:

- Brown rice
- Peas
- Wheat
- Milk
- Strawberries
- Spinach
- Corn

They should avoid sugar and starch.

LIBRA AS A LOVER

Male

Most loveable lover. He is sincere and affectionate, with charming manners. He is dress and fashion conscious and attracts the opposite sex. His passions rise and die quickly. He has a compromising nature. The partner should be sophisticated, well-groomed and tactful to be happy with him. He is a lazy lover unconcerned with the practical details of life.

He is compatible with:

Aries:	Sex but not marriage, friendship.
Leo:	Physically an excellent union.
Libra:	A great friendship and sex.
Sagittarius:	Physically an excellent union.
Aquarius:	Romance, marriage, business and lasting friendship.

He is incompatible with:

Cancer
Scorpio
Capricorn
Pisces

Female

She is intelligent, tactful and wise. Passionate in nature, she loves and adores her partner. Fond of dress, music, dance, restaurants, clubs, etc. Cannot be imposed upon. Emotional and extravagant, amiable and ready to forgive and forget.

She is compatible with:

Gemini:	Romance, love, marriage, business and long lasting friendship.
Sagittarius:	Physically an excellent union.

She is incompatible with:

Taurus
Cancer
Leo
Virgo

YOUR RELATIONSHIPS

Libra with Libra

There is no conflict when Air mixes with Air and, since they are both ruled by Venus, the planet of peace, harmony, balance and beauty, it will be easy to agree on most things. Discord or conflict really upsets Librans, so each will avoid or leave unfinished anything likely to cause this. They are both easy going and lack a fighting spirit, so they do not make a very progressive team.

Astro Advice

- The man should curb his habit of over-spending.
- The woman should wear light-coloured clothes.

Libra with Scorpio

Venus and masculine Mars can create a strong physical, emotional and sexual attraction. However gentle Libra may find the intensity and severity of Scorpio overwhelming at times. The secret of happiness is that each is keen to find something to share which gives pleasure and satisfaction to both. Libra is tactful enough not to provoke the Scorpion's sting. There is a mutual attraction between Libra's charming allure and Scorpio's sex appeal.

Astro Advice

- The woman should wear pearl of three rattis on Monday.
- The man should trust his beloved.

Libra with Sagittarius

Air will harmonise well with Fire in this combination, because the union of their ruling planets, Venus and Jupiter, increase their love, happiness, success and the ability to enjoy life. Libra needs to share things with someone special. Libra is tactful enough to allow need for freedom and independence. And Sagittarius is generous enough to allow Libra to indulge in little pleasures and luxuries.

Astro Advice

- The man should wear yellow sapphire of seven rattis on Thursday.
- The woman should wear white stone of four rattis on Monday.

Libra with Capricorn

Air does not easily combine with Earth, so there is likely to be some type of common purpose or destiny when these signs have a long-term association. Capricorn does not wear the heart on the sleeve and is unlikely to demonstrate openly the warmth of love and affection which Libra needs. Libra enjoys ease, luxury and self-indulgence. Capricorn's attitude of taking life seriously attracts responsibility and thus can cope with austerity much better than Libra, if it is necessary. Capricorn should remember that sharing love, affection and beautiful things is as vital to Libra as food and water.

Astro Advice

- The woman should dress up in traditional wear, with a matching bindi on her forehead.
- The man should avoid dreaminess.

Libra with Aquarius

Air harmonises with Air, therefore these two signs are naturally friendly and need the company of each other and can share pleasures together. Libra is the epitomé of the personal lover, whereas Aquarius is the universal lover who needs to share interests and affections with many people. Aquarius has an unpredictable attitude so Libra uses tact and diplomacy, rather than anger, to handle the situation. Neither will make impossible demands on the other, yet they can have togetherness if Libra allows Aquarius freedom.

Astro Advice

- The man should avoid fickle love.
- The woman should realise that sweet words work like a magic cure on her beloved.

Libra with Pisces

The harmony between their ruling planets, Jupiter and Neptune, helps bridge the gap between Air and Water. Although they are different in nature, there can be an affinity because both appreciate beauty, the arts, entertainment, harmony, gentleness, love, affection, togetherness and the magic of romance. Libra's innate sense of balance and judgement will help counteract Piscean's confusion, indecision and impracticality.

Astro Advice

- The woman should respond vibrantly to the feelings and ideas of her beloved.
- The man should improve his tolerance power.

ASTRO GUIDE

How to improve your luck

Lucky Date: All series of 6 and 15th.

Lucky Day: Friday for meetings, Sunday for love and romance.

Lucky Colour: Blue, royal blue; these should be used as curtains, bed sheets and as colour of wall. Attire should also match lucky colour.

Lucky Gem: Diamond or sapphire between 3-4 rattis to be worn on Friday morning after pran pratishtha.

Lucky Metal: Silver, platinum, aluminium.

Mantra: Aum Hran Hrin Hron Se: Shukraye Namah.

Lucky Talisman: Scale, key or shoe made of silver platinum to be worn next to skin.

SCORPIO

THE SCORPION

(24th October – 22nd November)
The Sign of the King or President

- Governs the sexual and reproductive organs.
- Planetary Ruler: Mars.
- Virtues: Strong-willed, bold, frank, and energetic.
- Vices: Sarcastic, over-critical, rash-tempered.

SCORPIO (SUN SIGN)

Scorpions are ruled by the planet Mars which is hot, fiery, passionate and stubborn. Scorpions are tireless workers as well as incredible extremists. They work very hard – sometimes too hard – trying to control their emotions. They are amazing workaholics and the more challenges they accept, the more outlets they will have for all their energy. They are extremely determined, business-oriented and possess a fertile imagination and sharp intelligence. They have deep intuition, powerful emotions and extremely high standards, which they set for themselves and others.

Persons born during this period are determined, independent and energetic. They have a magnetic personality and are versatile. Paradoxically, the basest and noblest of persons are found in this sign. Scorpios usually lead a double life, one for themselves and another for others. They have clear ideas about business and politics. Scorpio makes successful physicians, surgeons, detectives, researchers, psychiatrists and military officers. They are very demanding in their sex life, and are dogmatic and dominating at home. They have as many friends as enemies.

They have strong likes and dislikes and cannot be persuaded easily to change plans and opinions. Scorpios have an inflexible will power and great self-reliance and this may be one of the reasons why they do not trust or rely on other people.

They are willing to work hard and long to achieve their goal and, being secretive, do not normally divulge all their plans. They may tell some of the facts but they always keep their trump card hidden.

Any trouble they may experience in life are likely to be the result of too much emotional intensity or jealousy.

They have command of language, both in speaking and writing, and are intensively dramatic in their power of description.

They are mental fighters. They make good organisers if forced into warfare, but as a rule they detest bloodshed.

Both the best and the worst in this sign are inclined in one way or another to lead to some form of a 'double life' – one for the eyes of the world and the other for themselves. They are generally loved and adored by those who know them, but there are very few born under this sign who at some stage in their career escape from being attacked by some insidious form of calumny or scandal.

SCORPIO (MOON SIGN)

VRISHCHIK (To, N, Ni, Nu, Ne, Ya, Ye, Yu)

Scorpio (Vrishchik), symbolised by Scorpion, is energetic, independent and passionate. If born during early hours or sunset it is unfortunate, since it gives tendency towards perjury and robs the native of any good attributes. He cannot shake off his inner inclinations towards deceit, indolence or excessiveness. These may be attired by favourable influences, however there shall be too many problems to conquer – ill-luck and a life marked with diseases and threats of all types.

Such a situation is not good for women and signifies barrenness, at time miscarriages, provided Mars is weak.

From the moral standpoint the native is self-confident, brave, energetic and enduring. Scorpios know what they want and will do anything to get it. They have a critical mind, which immediately senses what others think. It is difficult to deceive them, for they are intuitive and observant. This position gives them fine possibilities of succeeding through their own industry, knowledge and skill. With Mercury on the cusp of the ascendant, they will make remarkably good businessmen; while a good position of Mars will make them a banker or financier who will have to be reckoned with.

A Scorpio's eagle eye can serve him well for it may prevent him from rushing into a hasty marriage. The native can definitely recognise his or her future spouse on sight, nevertheless they will still wait and watch before taking the final plunge.

SCORPIO – YOUR PERSONAL OUTLOOK

The Scorpio-born has a well-set body and a medium stature. They have a youthful appearance and a fickle mind. They are clever, powerful and dignified. They are cruel, sensual and usually not generous. A Scorpio native is a good conversationalist and possesses equally good writing skills. Spouse will be polite and flexible.

A Scorpio will have the following characteristics:

- Dark complexion
- Thick curly hair
- Thick eyebrows
- Aquiline nose
- Fleshy or dumpy body

SCORPIO – YOUR OCCULT FOUNDATION

Scorpio is ruled by Mars, whose occult value is nine. The number nine has polarised positive and negative associations. In its positive aspects nine is the number of spiritual and mental achievement. The Hebrews considered it to be the number of truth, because when multiplied it reproduces itself. In Kabbalism, it represents the foundation. As the triple Triad, it is the incorruptible number of fulfillment and attainment. In the Eleusinian mysteries, there were nine spheres through which the consciousness had to pass before it could be born anew. It is also a number of man, symbolising the nine months of gestation before birth. Because of its composition of equal threes, nine has associations with the triangle.

The Pythagoreans regarded nine as an evil number because it is an inverted six, and also regarded it as the number of imperfection and failure, because it falls one short of the perfect ten. Within this context, nine is the number of limitations.

FINANCE AND PROFESSION

Scorpios deal with chemistry, medicine, insurance, maternity department, surgery, research work, iron and steel work, military and naval department. They can be good politicians, orators and composers of great musical works, and can be actors and dramatists.

As a rule they will be successful in whatever they undertake after a hard uphill fight in the early years. They may be expected to overcome all obstacles and difficulties and gain money and position.

They are hard workers and their sense of purpose in life makes them serious in making money. They have an excellent business sense and generally handle high finance. They could be physicians, chemists, doctors, detectives, spiritualists, military leaders, etc. They make excellent hypnotists and surgeons.

HEALTH AND FOOD

They have a strong constitution with phenomenal stamina. They will be liable to fever of all kinds, high blood pressure and overstraining of the heart. They are prone to accidents, chiefly those caused by machines, and also from firearms. They are likely to meet violent mobs who can create injuries on their head and brain. The sex organs, throats, tonsils are the sensitive health zones. Drugs and drinks should be avoided at all costs. Health seeking habits are prominent. Their cell salt is Calcium Sulphate used in the repair of tissues.

The following food should be included in their diet:

- Onion
- Mustard
- Cabbage
- Cauliflower
- Fish
- Cereals
- Honey
- Radish
- Green vegetables
- Coconut

SCORPIO AS A LOVER

Male

Rash in temperament, but of adjustable nature. Intense, dynamic in romance and love but of complex moods. Cannot tolerate any criticism. He should be given sympathy, good understanding and steady affection to enjoy sex and love. Valiant and of fixed views.

He is compatible with:

Virgo:	A good relationship.
Pisces:	Romance, marriage, business and lasting friendship.

He is incompatible with:

Aries
Taurus
Leo

Sagittarius
Capricorn
Aquarius

Female

She enjoys life if her partner shows genuine affection and deep love. Otherwise she might suddenly lose her temper and pounce upon her spouse or lover without caring for his passion, so why not avoid this to lead a harmonious life? She is very passionate and ardent in love.

She is compatible with:

Taurus:	Friendship, sex but not marriage.
Cancer:	Romance, marriage, business and lasting friendship.
Scorpio:	Physically an excellent union.
Pisces:	Romance, marriage, business and lasting friendship.

She is incompatible with:

Gemini
Libra
Sagittarius
Aquarius

YOUR RELATIONSHIPS

Scorpio with Scorpio

This double combination of the emotional element, Water, will intensify the already strong feelings, desires, emotions and passions which are either latent or active in every Scorpio. There are no half measures with the sign, so two people with such purpose and driving force will achieve great things if goals agree. If not, violent clashes are likely. There is a touch of both the saint and the devil in this combination.

Astro Advice

- The man should keep cunning and falsehood at bay.
- The woman should not compare her beloved with anyone.

Scorpio with Sagittarius

Unless they compromise, this combination of Water with Fire can create problems. The Sagittarian's independence and need to feel free will arouse Scorpio's jealousy when the latter's desire to possess anything is denied. Scorpio demands much of both – self and others – but Sagittarius will rebel against being controlled, dominated or forced in any way. The Sagittarian's enthusiasm can bring out the best in Scorpio. Scorpio, being secretive, seldom divulges all that he or she thinks. This trait will fascinate, irritate or mystify the naturally frank Sagittarian.

Astro Advice

- The man should wear yellow sapphire of six rattis.
- The woman should wear pearl of four rattis.

Scorpio with Capricorn

Water harmonises with Earth, but since their rulers are the 'tough' planets, Mars and Saturn, neither of them expects life to be an easy road or full of fun and games. Both signs can be dedicated, determined and hardworking. Where important goals are involved in serious or practical matters, they make a good team if their objectives coincide. When conflicts arise, they can be deadly enemies, since neither of them readily gives up. Serious rifts will not be easily or quickly resolved in this pairing.

Astro Advice

- The man should avoid being materialistic.
- The woman should keep no secret. If she shares her problem, she will find a solution.

Scorpio with Aquarius

The lack of affinity between Water and Air is the great difference between these signs. They are both strong-willed and determined, so if they can channel their combined forces into a common goal, great achievements are possible. Scorpio is intensely emotional and naturally possessive, but Aquarius likes to feel uncluttered and free to share interests, activities, affection with friends, groups and social causes. If Scorpio tries to possess and dominate the indomitable Aquarian, it will bring rebellion.

Astro Advice

- The man should realise that his beloved expects much from him; so he should get ready for it.
- The woman should be tactful and laconic.

Scorpio with Pisces

There is a magnetic attraction between these two Water signs and in combination they will generate an intensely emotional relationship. Scorpio has an inborn desire to dominate or conquer something or someone, so needs the other to succumb. Pisces can give Scorpio the impression of being submissive but, in reality, often it is a devious manoeuvre. Pisces can soothe and anaesthetise the inner tensions, compelling desires and compulsive striving within Scorpio. Each intuitively senses the other's moods, needs, fears and faults. When things go wrong, an overabundance of emotions will cloud the issue and mar settlement.

Astro Advice

- The man should lap up flattery.
- The woman should give extra attention to her beloved.

ASTRO GUIDE

How to improve your luck

Lucky Date: 1st, 4th, 10th, 13th, 19th, 22nd, 31st.

Lucky Day: Sunday for meetings, Thursday for love and romance.

Lucky Colour: Red, orange and white. These should used as curtains, bed sheets and as colour of wall. Attire should also match lucky colour.

Lucky Gem: Ruby or amber to be worn on Sunday morning before 8:00 a.m.

Lucky Flower: Red rose, sunflowers, rosemary.

Mantra: Aum Hran Hrin Hron Se: Suryaye Namah.

Lucky Talisman: Sun in gold to be worn next to skin.

SAGITTARIUS

THE ARCHER

(23rd November – 21st December)
The Sign of the Sage or Counsellor

Governs the hips and thighs.
Planetary Ruler: Jupiter.
Virtues: Generous, bold, good-hearted.
Vices: Restless, extravagant, greedy.

SAGITTARIUS (SUN SIGN)

Sagittarius is symbolised by the Centaur – half-horse and half-man who is always pictured pointing his bow and arrow towards the sky. Eternally optimistic and hopeful about the future, Sagittarians try to persuade others to develop the same attitude. They are always searching for the key to knowledge and happiness without working too hard to attain it. They have very high principles and are sometimes frank to the point of being painfully brutal. They have a joy and enthusiasm for life and a love of sports, travelling to foreign countries, learning and teaching. They enjoy meeting foreigners and very often live abroad or marry foreigners.

Persons born during this period are enthusiastic, determined and impulsive. They are usually outspoken and thus make many enemies. Being honest themselves, Sagittarians resent deception. They are friendly and sociable. They usually go to extremes in all things and make sudden decisions. However they are successful at whatever they do. They are best suited to a career connected with teaching, writing, publishing, research, defense and sports. They usually marry on impulse and are seldom happy in their married life.

Another strongly marked characteristic which naturally accompanies their driving urge to expand is a strong sense of independence and a great love of freedom. They will not tolerate anyone or anything restricting their freedom or placing limitations on their thoughts or actions. As a matter of fact this particular zodiacal influence on the ascendant is found in people who have strong love affairs, romance with unconventional people or those who have married more than once.

Of course, it can also cause the other extreme where the person refuses to give up his or her freedom and does not marry at all. Naturally where the success or failure or marriage is concerned, the influence of the Sun, Moon and the planets must be considered. Certainly not every person with Sagittarius on the ascendant is destined for a broken marriage but, nevertheless, it is an influence which needs careful handling.

They concentrate all their attention in whatever they are doing at the moment, and see no other way until their effort is spent.

Their minds are so quick in thoughts that they will be often found breaking in on the conversation of others and show their impatience with slow or ponderous speakers. They are inclined to make sudden decisions for which they may have regrets, but they will be too proud to acknowledge their errors. They are staunch upholders of law and order and regularly visit places of worship, holy places and old archaeological spots.

SAGITTARIUS (MOON SIGN)

DHANU (Ye, Yo, Bh, Bhi, Bhu, Dh, Ph, Th, Bhe)

This sign endows great mental and physical compatibility. It signifies an unworldly mind, idealism and carelessness with attire. It signifies a disregard for finances and wealth, however the native will never lack these since the Moon frequently gets legacies while in the Sign. Prosperity is indicated through the native who shall help her partner morally, financially and mentally. There may be hardship and strenuous labour, however the desired consequences shall always be reached. It promises a big and harmonious domestic circle.

Persons in this sign are bestowed with great confidence, excellent ability of the divine and a tendency to conserve which will enable the native to live a long life, particularly those born in early morning or late evening.

The native is affectionate, devoted and generous, and knows how to win the love of those around him; he will be ready to risk his fortune and even his life, if he judges that those in whom he takes an interest are worth it. He is extremely logical and benevolent.

This position gives a taste for travelling, a love of philosophy, and enables the native to succeed as a government official, or a director. His mind is essentially materialistic, but this does not prevent him from being interested in religion or philosophy in its practical aspects.

SAGITTARIUS – YOUR PERSONAL OUTLOOK

The Sagittarius-born has a tall, corpulent body and attractive face. They are alert and intuitive. They have creative ability and are reliable. They have a high sense of honesty and justice. Spouse will be bad-tempered.

Sagittarius have the following characteristics:

- Tall and well-built
- Large nose
- Long face
- Clear but ruddy complexion

SAGITTARIUS – YOUR OCCULT FOUNDATION

Sagittarius is ruled by Jupiter, whose occult value is three. As the sum of one and two, three symbolises the generative force, creative power, multiplicity and forward movement. It is a spiritual synthesis, harmony, and sufficiency, also prudence, friendship, justice, peace, virtue and temperance. Anatolious observed that three, the first odd number, is called perfect by some, because it is the first number to signify the totality – beginning, middle, end. Thus we find in mythology, folklore, and fairy tales the recurrent motif of the triad – three wishes, three sisters, three brothers, three chances, blessings given in threes and spells and charms done in threes.

Three is also the number of wisdom and knowledge in its association with the three Fates and the past, present and future and the ancient sciences of music, geometry and arithmetic.

FINANCE AND PROFESSION

Can be a good teacher, orator, bank employee or politician. Attached to religious and educational institutions. Editing and publishing will be rewarding. They can also be a master of company law, civil engineer, contractor, or associated with foreign assignments. Speculation will not be helpful.

Jupiter is the ruling planet; they may certainly expect good fortune and generous slice of luck in money matters. They are sure to accumulate wealth in whatever work they are engaged in, but are inclined to take risks and at times lose heavily by speculation. They never blame others for their losses, but fall back on their work or profession and build up their bank balance again.

HEALTH AND FOOD

Generally they have splendid physical constitution and suffer very little from illness of any kind up to the age of about sixty. At this date, a change generally begins to show and if they do not lessen their responsibilities, the nervous system will begin to break down, in many cases bringing on some paralysis affecting the spine, arms, hand and brain. Over-work should be avoided and they should focus on complete rest and spiritualism.

The following food should be included in their diet:

- Raw eggs
- Raw vegetables

- Fruits
- Tomatoes
- Beans
- Corn

They should avoid spicy food and smoking.

SAGITTARIUS AS A LOVER

Male

The love of freedom and independence can cause a problem if the partner is a jealous or possessive lover. To make friends with all is his basic trait. He is more interested in outdoor life than home and family life. He has expensive tastes, encompassing vast visions, with a belief in spontaneous luck. He loves to travel for business, adventure or social work, etc.

He is compatible with:

Taurus:	A great friendship, sex.
Leo:	Romance, marriage, business and lasting friendship.
Libra:	Physically an excellent union.
Aquarius:	A great friendship sex.
Pisces:	Only a good sexual relationship.

He is incompatible with:

Gemini
Cancer
Scorpio
Capricorn

Female

She is fond of home and is non-interfering. She is helpful, calm, clever, polite and considerate. A reliable, intelligent, dutiful, obedient and pleasant person.

She is compatible with:

Aries:	Sex love, marriage, business and lasting friendship
Leo:	Romance, marriage, business and lasting friendship.
Libra:	Physically an excellent union.
Sagittarius:	Physically an excellent union.
Aquarius:	A great friendship, sex.

She is incompatible with:

Virgo
Scorpio
Pisces

YOUR RELATIONSHIPS

Sagittarius with Sagittarius

A combination of Fire and Fire is a most fortunate team which brings an atmosphere of enthusiasm and optimism with the Archer's honesty and exposure. The two of them spend lot of time analysing a matter which can cause delay, but once they are enlightened, Archers are capable of accomplishing when they work together towards a common goal. The women are friendly and cheerful, men are straightforward and optimistic, so majority of the couples are happy-go-lucky. It is a vibrational combination and so regardless of periodic conflict, they will remain friendly because of basic sympathy. They almost never become enemies even after they have exchanged heated words. Archers never hold grudges, forgiveness is their virtue.

Astro Advice

- The man should wear yellow sapphire of six rattis on Thursday.
- The woman should wear coral of five rattis on Tuesday.

Sagittarius with Capricorn

The marked contest between Fire and Earth is evident in this combination. Capricorn is cautious, conservative, prudent, serious and sometimes pessimistic. Sagittarius is exuberant, optimistic, impulsive and broad-minded. Even their ruling planets are opposites, because Jupiter symbolises expansion and exposure, whereas Saturn, the ruler of Capricorn, relates to contraction and limitation. Although opposites can attract, the differences in both their natures and outlook will certainly be manifest. Independent and freedom-loving Sagittarius will not take kindly to being repressed or restricted by Capricorn who, in turn, will not understand the Sagittarian's inner longings, high ideals and impossible dreams. If they can bridge the gap and achieve a happy relationship, each will certainly benefit in the long term.

Astro Advice

- The man should put on white shirt with black trousers while meeting his partner.
- The woman should remember that her hair is her crowning glory.

Sagittarius with Aquarius

There is a strong affinity between Fire and Air, as well as between their rulers – Jupiter, (the God of thunder) and Saturn (the Lord of lightning). Each sign makes a strong impact on the other and yet, when necessary, they are willing to leave each other alone. They each have an independent streak and need freedom, so neither should trespass on the other's territory. Both signs have high ideals which transcend the personal level. These two signs are naturally friendly, so they will attract many people into their arena and share the resulting pleasures and reciprocal benefits.

Astro Advice

- The woman should trust her beloved.
- The man should be loyal to his beloved.

Sagittarius with Pisces

This combination of Fire with Water is full of complexities and presents a multitude of possibilities. For some, compatibility will be found in a mutual appreciation of philosophy, religion, mysticism, philanthropic pursuits, charitable causes, travel, humanitarian or other lofty ideas.

For others, there will be long periods of confusion, uncertainty or wishful thinking. In some cases each person may live in a private world, untouched and unnoticed by the others. Pisces' vivid imagination will probably conjure up the worst picture when Sagittarius feels the need to be independent. Although Sagittarius is basically kind, helpful and generous, the sign lacks the softness and tender loving care which is so essential to the hypersensitive Pisces. The Piscean tendency to be indecisive, impractical and disorganised may exasperate Sagittarius who is basically active, impulsive and positive and likes to get things done quickly and efficiently.

Astro Advice

- The man should look glamorous and charming while going to meet his beloved.
- The woman should remember financial insecurity is jeopardy.

ASTRO GUIDE

How to improve your luck

Lucky Date: All the series of 3 i.e. 3rd, 12th, 21st, 30th.

Lucky Day: Thursday for meetings, Monday for love and romance.

Lucky Colour: Yellow, off-white, orange; these should be used as colour of curtains, bed sheets and as colour of wall. Attire should also match lucky colour.

Lucky Gem: Pukhraj to be worn on the index finger on Thursday morning after Pran Pratishtha.

Lucky Metal: Gold.

Lucky Flower: Sunflowers, pink rose.

Mantra: Gran Grien Gron Se: Gurvey Namah.

Lucky Talisman: Gold archer to be worn next to skin.

CAPRICORN

THE GOAT

(22nd December – 20th January)
The Sign of the Priest or Scientist

Governs the knees.
Planetary Ruler: Saturn.
Virtues: Economical, prudent, self-willed and reserved.
Vices: Selfish, egoistic, pessimistic, nervous.

CAPRICORN (SUN SIGN)

In accordance with their symbol of the Goat, Capricornians have immense organisational skill and an overwhelming desire and ability to achieve their goals at any cost. Whatever Capricornians set out to do will be followed through to the end despite many obstacles along the way.

Persons born during this period are mentally strong, determined, hardworking and independent in all their actions. They can excel in any work that requires administrative or managerial skills, including government service, commerce, agriculture, engineering and education. They neither interfere in the affairs of others, nor tolerate interference by others. Their temperament is somewhat melancholic and, therefore generally misunderstood by others. Family life of Capricornians is usually troubled.

They are economical, frugal, cautious and very rarely proceed without planning in advance. They are good and loyal friends, honest, upright and persevering to a fault without ever complaining. They are faithful and extremely good providers but need secure homes to which they can always return and reflect upon their busy lives. They are born leaders and possess great executive abilities.

Capricornians can be extremely disciplined and calculating to the point of ruthlessness.

Perseverance is a keyword of their nature. Once they decide to reach a goal they will persist until they do so. It may take some time to decide just what they want to do in life but once they reach a decision, their steadfast determination will help them achieve almost anything they want to.

They are not the type who live just for the moment; they plan for the future, are economical and wherever possible their financial affairs are organised to ensure comfort and security in both – their prime of life and later years.

Being influenced by Saturn they are neither flippant nor superficial but rather serious minded, patient, thrifty and stable. These are excellent qualities but they should be careful not to allow an over-cautious attitude to cramp their initiative and so prevent them from taking a chance to expand.

A Capricornian's outlook is practical and down-to-earth and there is likely to be a lack of imagination and fun in their nature. They should cultivate their sense of humour and not allow an over-serious and pessimistic outlook to overrule the joy of living.

They are quick in their intuition of people and things but are inclined to be too easily discouraged in their plans and fall into a despondent state at the first rebuff or disappointment. Their views on love, duty or social economics will be always unique, faithful and honest.

As a general rule they will be misunderstood by others. They will not easily mix with people. They will have a few close friends, but at heart feel very much alone.

CAPRICORN (MOON SIGN)

MAKAR (Gu, Ge, Go, Sa, Si, Su, Se, So, D)

Capricorn (Makar) symbolised by Goat is impartial, just and precise. The native succeeds in bringing perfection and economic stability. Saturn will restrict his progress and his efforts will take him long to achieve his goal. He will rise through his own merits and success will normally come late in life.

Morally, Capricorn chiefly denotes an exaggerated sense of independence, craftiness, shrewdness in small matters, patience and often leading to a meagre result, especially in the initial period of life. Later on, if the horoscope on the whole is favourable, Capricorn on the ascendant procures success in politics or business due to cunning.

To some extent external influences will affect his friendship, union and general success. Striving to remove unpleasantness from his surroundings, the Capricornian will excel in patching up misunderstandings.

In advancing years he is usually looked up to as an authority on matters of consultancy. This character remembers and observes dates of anniversaries making much of a special occasion beside being a delightful quest. Overall a silent lover, good parent and a generous human being, popular among friends.

CAPRICORN – YOUR PERSONAL OUTLOOK

Capricorn persons are of middle-stature, clever and fickle. They are able to adapt themselves according to circumstances. They are strong-minded and very patient. They will have few children. Spouse will be attractive and happy-go-lucky.

A Capricornian will have the following characteristics:

- Average stature
- Short, slight and bony figure
- Long nose
- Sharp face
- Thin chin
- Straight hair

CAPRICORN – YOUR OCCULT FOUNDATION

Capricorn is ruled by Saturn, whose occult value is eight. The number of regeneration and the spiritual goal of the initiate. Because of its association with regeneration, eight symbolised the water of baptism during the Middle Ages.

On its side, the figure eight resembles an ellipse, which is the symbol of eternity, infinity, the alpha and omega, infinite wisdom and higher consciousness. Right side up, the eight is associated with a spiral, a shape representing evolution, growth and flexibility. The serpents entwined in a spiral on the caduceus of Hermes represents transformed consciousness, spiritual illumination. Thus it is not surprising that the number eight was important in the Eleusinian mysteries.

FINANCE AND PROFESSION

In spite of meeting great opportunities, they are not likely to make much provision for their failing years. Although capable of giving splendid advice to others, they will not follow it for their own personal advantage. To the surprise of their friends, towards the end of their days they are likely to become comparatively poor by giving their money away to others or making peculiar provisions in their will. They need to exercise great prudence and care if they are to keep their position and wealth.

They can be contractors, cement brokers, dealers in scientific instruments, physicians, and gain through lands, mines, kerosene or petrol, chemicals, etc.

HEALTH AND FOOD

In health, sudden and unexpected illness is likely to happen. Stoppages and strictures of the internal organs and operations may be expected, but against this there will be long periods of good health.

They should study all questions of diet more than the average person and not stay for any length of time in damp low-lying districts.

They are liable to have injuries on the lower limbs, weakness or turning of the ankles, injuries to the spinal column caused by falls or by accidents. Though the Saturnine influence indicates Virgo's constitution and good physical stamina, in Capricorn's case, their tendency to depression may cause complicated health problems. They should cultivate optimism and cheerful disposition in order to keep in good health.

The following food should be included in their diet:

- Figs
- Green vegetables
- Cow's milk
- Oranges
- Lemons
- Egg yolk
- Cheese
- Fish
- Food grains

CAPRICORN AS A LOVER

Male

He is not emotional, but slow and cautious. He is not bold in approaching the opposite sex and not demonstrative in love. He is a dependable, sturdy and practical lover. He is materalistic and often overcome by his love and affection for money. Public display of affection is not liked by him.

He is compatible with:

Taurus:	Romance, sex, marriage, business and long lasting friendship.
Virgo:	Romance, sex, marriage and long lasting friendship.
Pisces:	Friendship and sex but not marriage.

He is incompatible with:

Gemni
Leo
Aquarius
Pisces

Female

She is much attached to home and family and dutiful to children. She does not display her love and hates any adverse publicity or any hint of discord in her private life. She is conservative.

She is compatible with:

Virgo: Romance, sex, marriage, business and long lasting friendship.
Capricorn: A great friendship, sex.

She is incompatible with:

Gemini
Libra
Scorpio
Sagittarius
Aquarius

YOUR RELATIONSHIPS

Capricorn with Capricorn

The double dose of Earthy Capricornians multiply their cautious, conservative, realistic approach to life. It is important to have contact with other type of people or they both will take things too seriously and will miss out on many light-hearted pleasures. If they are working towards the same objectives, their combined ambitions and perseverance will ensure success, However if one tries to use the other for selfish ends, it can lead to much bitterness and resentment. Outsiders who are more adventurous and relaxed are likely to find this Capricorn duo too serious and formal.

Astro Advice

- The man should avoid junk food and focus on exercise.
- The woman should observe silence over heated discussions.

Capricorn with Aquarius

There is little in common between Earth and Air or between their respective rulers – cautious Saturn and unpredictable, orthodox Uranus. This relationship will be subject to changes of mood, routine and attitudes. Many personal readjustments will have to be made on both sides, although these may not be easy to achieve because Aquarius is independent and stubborn about personal ideas, while Capricorn is tenacious, holding tight to goals and convictions.

Astro Advice

- The man should wear black stone of five rattis on the ring finger.
- The woman should wear blue sapphire of four rattis on Saturday.

Capricorn with Pisces

Earth has an affinity with Water and although there is a great difference between these signs, they do complement each other. Pisces finds it easy to amalgamate and can adapt to people and situations which are safe and secure. Capricorn is the epitomé of safety and security. Pisces is intensely sensitive, emotional, romantic and sentimental, so may feel sad or hurt when Capricorn hides his or her true feelings.

Astro Advice

- The man should wear blue sapphire of four rattis on Saturday.
- The woman should focus on good habits.

ASTRO GUIDE

How to improve your luck

Lucky Date: 8th, 17th, 26th.
Lucky Day: Saturday for meetings, Tuesday for love and romance.
Lucky Colour: Black, grey and dark brown/blue. These should be used as curtains, bed sheets and as colours of wall. Attire should also match lucky colour.
Lucky Gem: Neelam and dark sapphire. It should be worn on Saturday morning after Pran Pratishtha.
Lucky Metal: Iron, steel and aluminium.

Lucky Flower: Ivy and pansies.
Mantra: Aum Aien Hrin Sri: Shancharye Namah.
Lucky Talisman: Ring of horse shoe.

AQUARIUS

THE WATER BEARER

(21st January – 19th February)
The Sign of the Truth-Seeker or Inventor

Governs the calves and ankles.
Planetary Ruler: Saturn.
Virtues: Honest, probing, broad-minded.
Vices: Jealous, prejudiced, critical, stuffy.

AQUARIUS (SUN SIGN)

Aquarius, an Air sign, is often mistaken for a Water sign since it is symbolised by someone carrying the waters of humanity and pouring it over the earth. The element Air represents the desire to communicate brotherhood and freedom to the rest of the world. Aquarians have inventive minds and are always seeking innovative projects in which they may become involved. They are socially conscious and are identified with groups fighting social and political injustice. Interests range from technology, to astrology and social work.

Persons born during this period are over-sensitive and their feelings are easily hurt. They often lose control of themselves and say or do things which they regret later. Though they are sociable, they suffer from loneliness in life. They do, however, make good friends and wise counsellors. Persons with Aquarius as their Sun Sign are successful at debates and arguments. They have a scientific bent of mind and are successful as doctors, writers, actors, scientists and psychologists. They take great interests in public meetings and ceremonies. In their personal life, they often indulge in clandestine love affairs and are unhappy in their married life.

They have a straightforward temperament and disposition which is liked by most people. An easy and genuine friendliness comes naturally, and their friendships are often long and many in number. Yet, strangely, no matter how well or how long a person has been associated with them, he or she never comes to know them completely. This stems from the complex and unfathomed depths which are latent in the sign of Aquarius. Of course, the average person does not realise this and interprets it as a pleasant aloofness in their nature. They give the impression of being slightly detached, without appearing unfriendly or unsympathetic.

They love meeting new people with whom they can exchange ideas, and always enjoy surroundings themselves with others dedicated to the same ideals. They have difficulties being intimate with one person because of their involvement with groups and causes. Their shortcomings include a highly strung nature, impatience and an inflexibility to change habits and patterns which would put their lives on a more even keel.

They will not be demonstrative in their affections or able to express their love; they will however be intensely loyal to those they love and will fight to the bitter end for a friend or for any cause they espouse.

They have strong intuitions about those they come in contact with and will be generally right in their judgement. They will read people instinctively but being sensitive and so disclaimed to hurt others, they will be prone to conceal their opinion or keep it to themselves.

They will have remarkably good ideas in business and will be found giving excellent advice to others but as a general rule they will find themselves unsuccessful due to lack of initiative.

AQUARIUS (MOON SIGN)

KUMBH (Ghu, Ghe, Gho, Sa, Si, Su, Se, So, D)

The persons born under this sign are honest, probing and broad-minded. The Moon bestows a melancholy, profound and sombre temperament. The native enjoys being by himself and is generally compassionate. However, life's disillusionments may make him distressful of mankind.

This placement brings about an inclination to carry out impossible and impractical, idealistic inquiries which may bring misfortune. The preference and thoughts of the native are strange, more so if Saturn is badly aspected in which case, the mental state of the native may cause anxiety.

When influenced in a beneficial manner, the Moon in Aquarius endows the native with an imagination that runs in wild and depressive directions. His life will be morose and morbid and this will be his own doing.

However in spite of all this, this situation of the Moon brings appreciation from the female sex, especially born during the day time. However these alliances will be temporary, strange and ill-matched which may cause speculative rumours in society.

From the moral standpoint Aquarius gives benevolence, cheerfulness and liveliness. The native is impulsive, energetic and enterprising; he is gifted with fine intellectual and practical qualities, and has a strong personality. He knows exactly what he wants, his ideas are firmly established, and may incline him to be self-opinionated. He has a good chance of success in politics or in some prominent position. He may also have a taste for the fine arts, and if the horoscope on the whole confirms it, may progress in this direction.

AQUARIUS – YOUR PERSONAL OUTLOOK

The Aquarius-born is of middle-stature and strong. They are talkative, happy and stubborn. They are kind and fond of learning. Spouse will be ill-tempered.

They have the following characteristics:

- Well-formed body
- Ruddy complexion
- Brown eyes
- Oval shaped face

AQUARIUS – YOUR OCCULT FOUNDATION

Aquarius is ruled by Saturn whose occult value is four. The number of solidity, stability, foundations, hard work and toil, and tangible achievement – four. It is also the number of the Earth, and of rational and logical thought and intellectualism. Pythagoras considered four the perfect number, the foundation of all things, connecting beings, elements, numbers and seasons. To the Pythagoreans, four also symbolised God, because when added to the first three numbers, the total is ten, which turns to one. In addition, they believed that four represented the soul of man, which had the four powers of mind, science, opinion and sense.

Many things can be associated with four: the four seasons, the four elements, the four cardinal points, the four basic functions of Jungian types (thinking, feeling, sensation and intuition), the four suits of the tarot, the four limbs of the human body, the four rivers that flow from the Garden of Eden.

FINANCE AND PROFESSION

Persons born in this sign can always make money, provided they apply themselves to that one purpose. They will however be liable to lose money by actions caused by the opposite sex or by litigation and blackmail.

Politics fascinate them. They can be connected with sports, automobiles, meuical discoveries, writing and can be astronauts, pianists.

HEALTH AND FOOD

Persons born in this sign give the appearance of being more healthy than they really are. They get little or no warning about illness. They often suddenly collapse from heart failure or a blood clot in the brain.

The following food should be included in their diet:

- Fish
- Pear

- Lemon
- Oranges
- Radish
- Grapes
- Peach

AQUARIUS AS A LOVER

Male

Being intelligent, he prefers an equally intelligent partner. This sexy, interesting and cosmopolitan lover may seldom be available for the partner alone. He is popular and very much in demand. Some of them like love to be on a romantic and impersonal basis. He prefers permanent and strong attachment. He is cold and does not show love.

He is compatible with:

Sagittarius: A great friendship, sex.

He is incompatible with:

Scorpio
Capricorn
Pisces

Female

She is unconventional. In case she finds that her partner is not up to her standard, she will not hesitate to satisfy herself by changing the partner. Otherwise she will cooperate fully.

She is compatible with:

Aries:	A long friendship.
Libra:	Romance, marriage, business and lasting friendship.
Aquarius:	Physically an excellent union.
Sagittarius:	A great friendship, sex.

She is incompatible with:

Taurus
Gemini
Leo
Scorpio
Capricorn

YOUR RELATIONSHIPS

Aquarius with Aquarius

The Air sign Aquarius is ruled by Saturn, the planet of all that is original, unique, inventive, erratic, unusual, unorthodox and wayward. Outsiders may not be able to fathom this complex Aquarian's wavelength because it takes one Aquarian to know another. Much will depend on which of the many facets of this sign each person reflects but, sooner or later, unusual, surprising, changeable or disruptive conditions will affect this partnership.

Astro Advice

- The man should emphasise spiritualism.
- The woman should avoid long-term plans.

Aquarius with Pisces

It would be hard to find a more unusual combination than Airy Aquarius with Watery Pisces, for the simple reason that their respective rulers – Saturn and Jupiter – are 'out of the world', beyond the boundary lines of Uranus. Consequently, they transcend the limits of personal ideas and give unique qualities which others do not possess. They are both different from most people and sometimes feel misfits, except with other Aquarians and Pisceans.

Astro Advice

- The woman should sense the potential of her partner and look forward to what's ahead.
- The man should be confident while speaking and avoid flirtation.

ASTRO GUIDE

How to improve your luck

Lucky Date:	8th, 17th, 26th.
Lucky Day:	Saturday for meetings, Thursday for love and romance.
Lucky Colour:	Black, grey and blue. These should be used as curtains, bed sheets and as colour of wall. Attire should also match lucky colour.
Lucky Gem:	Neelam. It should be worn on Saturday morning after Pran Pratishtha.

Lucky Metal: Iron, steel and aluminium.
Lucky Flower: Ivy and pansies.
Mantra: Aum Aein Hrin Sri: Shancharya Namah.
Lucky Talisman: Ring of horse shoe.

PISCES

THE FISH

(20th February – 20th March)
The Sign of the Poet or Interpreter

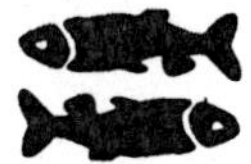

Governs the feet.
Planetary Ruler: Jupiter.
Virtues: Easy-going, good-natured and adaptable.
Vices: Suspicious, too emotional and overliberal.

PISCES (SUN SIGN)

The zodiac sign of Pisces is ruled by Jupiter, which symbolises Fish. The character of this individual sign is most difficult to determine, as such it is inclined to be different from other signs. Its symbol is recognised by the two fishes attempting to swim in opposite directions while their tails are tied together and this signifies a dualistic character causing confusion to the people.

Persons born during this period are generous, sympathetic and kind. They have a tendency to brood and become melancholy. They are loyal to their friends or to any cause they take up, provided they feel they are trusted. They are generally successful in all positions of responsibility. Pisceans have a strong desire to love and be loved. Quite often, this leads them to carry on with a romance secretly.

There is honesty, love of the arts and an incredible empathy and compassion towards people. They lean towards cultivating a spiritual life and live abroad. They have vivid imagination and relate to the world through their feeling and instincts. Pisceans are sometimes incapable of making a decision due to a lack of faith in their own judgement. They do not always express themselves clearly, but are willing to help other people at a moment's notice.

At times Pisceans live in a world of their own creation and have difficulty facing reality. Their lack of clarity makes them difficult to understand, but they are nonetheless, extremely sensitive and incapable of hurting others. If they have hurt someone's feelings they tend to feel guilty and remorseful.

Pisceans are highly emotional. If they belong to the weak side, they are easily influenced by the people with whom they are thrown in contact, but if they belong to the stronger side, their emotional nature can lift them up to any position.

They are extremely sensitive and impressionable, with the result they can sense an atmosphere when they walk into a room. The only trouble is that they readily pick up and absorb other people's influences, so it is important for them to associate with the right kind of people, otherwise they could slip into the habit of doing as others do and thinking as others think. They are extremely sympathetic and unlikely to do anything to harm others. However, they should realise that it is sometimes necessary to be cruel in order to be kind.

They become disheartened at the slightest rebuff and, unless they make a determined effort to overcome their timidity, they will miss out on the rewards which the realisation of ideas would bring them. The whole nature of Pisces is receptive and negative; to counteract this they must train themselves to be more forceful, outgoing, practical and positive. Once they can do this they will have the best of both worlds: reality and romance.

PISCES (MOON SIGN)

MEEN (Di, Du, Th, Jh, De, Do, Ch, Chi)

Pisces (Meen) symbolised by Fish is a sign of gentleness and moody disposition. The Moon brings a craving for ease and luxury, laziness and a creative imagination, a whole lot of schemes but few implementations. In some cases it signifies indecisiveness and changeability in love, with greater appeal to the senses, and less of life and energy. If born in midday, the native is a chatterbox who either defames other people or is himself subject to defamation. He may either cheat others or be cheated himself. It signifies lack of interest in worldly ambition.

In 10° of Pisces, the Moon signifies a native who lies without realising it, who convinces himself that what he states is true and therefore, harms himself by doing so. Though in these degrees, the Moon has greater energy and life, it is also a definite indicator of unfaithfulness in matrimony.

When in 20° of Pisces, if the horoscope is good, the situation of the Moon is highly beneficial as it lets whatever is happening go on in an uninterrupted manner. However in case the horoscope is bad it will imply the converse.

The disposition is gentle (even indolent), incapable of reacting. The native takes things as they come. The native is good natured, slightly selfish without being spiteful, and shows affection and a readiness to render service to others, provided this does not require too much physical exertion. The native detests talking too much and anything that entails fatigue. Their indolence is only equalled by their reserve and self-centredness.

If the native has not inherited wealth, his position will be commonplace, but if he has means, the position makes a benevolent individual, who likes to help the weak. Pisces in the ascendant is favourable for domestic life, which is peaceful and calm. It may be conducive to a large family of children.

The native is inclined to be indifferent about restrictions and limitations provided the inner self is left free to feel, dream and grow according to its own nature.

PISCES – YOUR PERSONAL OUTLOOK

The Pisces-born has a symmetrical body. He is virtuous but lacks self-confidence. Though he is reserved, he is a trustworthy friend. He is educated, ambitious, and religious. He will have good tempered Spouse.

Pisceans will have the following characteristics:

- Round face
- Plump body
- Small and round nose
- Dreamy eyes

PISCES – YOUR OCCULT FOUNDATION

Pisces is ruled by Neptune, whose occult value is seven. Almost universally a sacred number, and the number of mystical man, for it is the sum of three and four, thus making the perfect order, representing the macrocosm. In alchemy, seven metals make up the Work, the alchemical transformation to the philosopher's stone. Seven is also the number of religion, the psychic, magic and luck. It is associated with clairvoyance and healing powers. In initiation, seven is the highest stage of illumination. In Hebrew symbolism it is the number of occult intelligence.

When the number seven occurs, it often indicates a search for wisdom, a growth of spirit, a need to rely upon intuition or to meditate on what has been learned. It also indicates a fondness for and harmony with nature.

FINANCE AND PROFESSION

They will be ambitious to make money but very careful about their name and reputation. They will gain by solid enterprise and have every likelihood of becoming wealthy. They will show an enterprising spirit in all that they undertake and will rise to prominence and position in whatever their career may be.

Can be successful as an accountant, banker, actor, businessman, liaison officer, managing director, organiser. They will be interested in music and opera houses, cinema, occult science. They could also work in the navy or shipping corporations. They could deal in drinks, beverage, cosmetics, chemicals, and be associated with a medical or educational department.

HEALTH AND FOOD

This question largely depends on their outlook on life. As long as they can continue in active work they will be healthy. If forced for any reason into inactivity they will become pleasure-loving and indolent, inclined to put on weight and let the reins of life easily drop from their hands.

The following food should be included in their diet:

- Egg yolk
- Onions
- Food grains
- Lamb
- Pears

PISCES AS A LOVER

Male

He remains attracted to a romantic life, prefers beauty in the partner and stays in the limelight. Suspicious by nature which kills his love, he likes flattery. He has his own dream world, one which is private and requires solitude. The need to be alone is very strong with him.

He is compatible with:

Aries:	Romantic, loving and strong friendship, good for marriage.
Taurus:	Sex and great friendship.
Gemini:	A shaky union for marriage but good for friendship and sex.
Cancer:	Sex, love and marriage.
Virgo:	Sex and great friendship.
Scorpio:	Romance, marriage, business and lasting friendship.

He is incompatible with:

Sagittarius

Female

Suspicious by nature, romantic and passionate. She is over-liberal and very generous. This should be avoided, so that she does not fall a victim to bad social elements and ruin her life. Sweet-tempered, polite, social she can be led away by fancies. She loves domestic life on the whole.

She is compatible with:

Taurus:	Sex and great friendship.
Cancer:	Sex, love and marriage.
Leo:	Physically, an excellent union.
Virgo:	Sex and great friendship.
Sagittarius:	Only a good sexual relationship.
Capricorn:	Friendship and sex but not marriage.

She is incompatible with:

Libra
Capricorn
Aquarius

YOUR RELATIONSHIPS

Pisces with Pisces

Because Pisces is a Water sign, feelings, emotions, intuition, daydreams, imagination and hypersensitivity to atmospheres are to the fore in this relationship and take precedence over logic and rational analysis. They both have their own private and secret world of make believe to escape to when necessary. They sense things about people, including each other, without a word being spoken. Both can become muddled, disorganised, indecisive and dither, so there will be periods when time is wasted and confusion reigns in practical matters.

Astro Advice

- The man should dress up in casual wear. Stripes suit him.
- The woman needs to be punctual.

ASTRO GUIDE

How to improve your luck

Lucky Date: 3rd, 12th, 21st, 30th.

Lucky Day: Thursday for meetings, Friday for love and romance.

Lucky Colour: Yellow; these should be used as curtains, bed sheets and as colour of wall. Attire should also match lucky colour.

Lucky Gem: Pukhraj and topaz to be worn on Thursday morning after Pran Pratishtha.

Lucky Metal: Gold.

Lucky Flower: Marigold.

Mantra: Aum Gran Grin Gron Shr Guravey Namah.

Lucky Talisman: Couple of fish.